SCIENTIFIC AMERICAN EXPLORES BIG IDEAS

The Science of Emotions

Published in 2026 by Scientific American Educational Publishing
in association with **The Rosen Publishing Group**
2544 Clinton Street, Buffalo NY 14224

Contains material from Scientific American®, a division of Springer Nature America, Inc., reprinted by permission, as well as original material from The Rosen Publishing Group®.

First Edition

Scientific American
Lisa Pallatroni: Project Editor

Rosen Publishing
Deanna Lepovich: Compiling Editor
Michael Moy: Senior Graphic Designer

Cataloging-in-Publication Data

Names: Scientific American, Inc.
Title: The science of emotions / edited by the Scientific American Editors.
Description: Buffalo, New York : Scientific American Educational Publishing, an imprint of Rosen Publishing, 2026. | Series: Scientific American explores big ideas | Includes glossary and index.
Identifiers: ISBN 9781538313138 (pbk.) | ISBN 9781538313145 (library bound) | ISBN 9781538313152 (ebook)
Subjects: LCSH: Emotions–Juvenile literature. | Emotion recognition–Juvenile literature. | Emotional intelligence–Juvenile literature.
Classification: LCC BF723.E6 S356 2026 | DDC 152.4–dc23

Manufactured in the United States of America
Websites listed were live at the time of publication.

Cover: useng/iStock.com and smx12/Shutterstock.com

CPSIA Compliance Information: Batch # CSSA26.
For Further Information contact Rosen Publishing at 1-800-237-9932.

CONTENTS

INTRODUCTION

Have you ever woken up in a bad mood for no reason, or had a case of spring fever so intense that you can't contain your joy? Emotions can be affected by a variety of factors, such as how well you sleep or what your environment is like.

Basic emotions, such as fear, anger, and happiness, are universal. They are felt by all humans, and even by animals. These universal emotions are temporary and can change seasonally, daily, and even hourly. How your emotions change can be based on the emotions of others around you, the type of situation or environment you are in, or the memories that surface in your mind. Learning to control these emotions allows us to dive deep into the information that they provide about ourselves and our relationships.

The articles in this book touch on various topics that will give you insight into your own emotions as well as those of the people around you. In Section 1, "Your Emotions and Other People," we learn how emotions influence how people feel and relate to others. This section also touches on emotional intelligence and how we read other people's emotions, whether correctly or incorrectly. In Section 2, "Emotions: Helpful or Not?," the articles selected discuss how even emotions we view as negative, such as anger, can motivate us and give us information about ourselves and the situations we find ourselves in. The third section, "Emotions and the Environment," is a more curious section, looking into the phenomenon of how your environment and nature play a role in how you are feeling, as well as a look at what we know about the emotions of some animals. In the last section, "Controlling Your Emotions," the selected articles give examples of how your emotions can be better regulated through your sleep, various physical and creative outlets, and by redirecting our initial responses. As you read through these articles, think about how your various emotions can all work together to improve how you go about your life.

Section 1: Your Emotions and Other People

Beliefs about Emotions Influence How People Feel, Act and Relate to Others

By Francine Russo

When I was a teenager, I declared that I did not *like* my grandma. My mother excoriated me not just for saying such a thing but for feeling it. That, in her eyes, made me a terrible person. She believed that. I tried not to.

Our beliefs about emotions–whether we feel that they're good or bad, controllable or uncontrollable, or useful or harmful–profoundly affect our life and relationships. Science has only recently committed itself to examining this issue, but it is now doing so with a vengeance. In 2020 the journal *Frontiers in Psychology* devoted an entire issue to everyday beliefs about emotion.

Why is all of this happening now? It all goes along with a growing interest in our response to moods and stress responses, says Stanford University psychologist James J. Gross. "I think this interest that's been cooking for the past couple of decades has been magnified by the pandemic," he says. "I think there's a growing awareness of how anxious and depressed and stressed so many of us are." He notes that there's a robust link between beliefs about the controllability of emotions and the use of emotion-regulation strategies to reduce anxiety and depression.

In just the past few years cutting-edge theorizing has focused more on the link between belief and emotion. And new empirical research has drilled down on the effects of specific beliefs. To begin with, a number of psychologists have created self-report scales. The Emotion Beliefs Questionnaire, for example, asks people how much they agree with statements such as "There is very little use for negative emotions" and "It doesn't matter how hard people try, they cannot change their positive emotions."Another scale, Individual Beliefs about Emotion (IBAE), focuses on more subjective variations such as "I don't want to admit to having certain feelings–but I know that I have them" and "If I let myself have some of these feelings, I fear I will lose control."

IBAE co-creator and University of Arkansas clinical psychologist Jennifer Veilleux finds this questionnaire helpful in therapy. If people think they should keep their feelings private, for example, they may not reveal these emotions, even in therapy. If so, they can't work on changing the feelings, she says.

Such beliefs matter. Research is showing that those who assume they can modify their emotions experience greater well-being both in the short and long term. If they feel sad or angry, for example, they can use an emotion-regulation strategy such as cognitive reappraisal to reduce their painful feelings.

Variously called reframing, reappraisal or rethinking, this popular technique has proved effective. A student who feels sad about their low grade, for example, can remind themselves that they didn't study much for that exam but that if they studied more next time, they'd be likely to do better. An employee who isn't promoted may consider how the advancement of a colleague with greater seniority was fair. The result is that there are fewer painful feelings such as sadness, anger or shame.

Another effective approach is learning to accept one's emotions without judging them. In a series of studies tracking acceptance and overall emotional health, University of Toronto psychologist Brett Q. Ford showed that accepting negative emotions led to better mental health. People were asked to keep a daily diary for two weeks. Each evening they reflected on the most stressful event that day and on their responses at the time and afterward. Six months later "acceptors" felt less depression and anxiety and more well-being overall. In a related lab experiment, how much subjects accepted versus judged their emotions was measured. Then each was asked to prepare and give a speech—"a time-worn way of inducing stress in the lab," Ford says. The higher their level of acceptance, she says, the less they felt anxiety, stress and worry.

While accepting your feelings is healthy, it may be even better to think of them as friends rather than foes. One experiment showed that people who viewed their emotions as more helpful than harmful in times of distress used effective strategies for moderating their emotions, showed less physiological reactivity during a stressful event (watching a disturbing film) and had greater overall well-being.

Which emotions do we see as our greatest friends? Perhaps unsurprisingly, people tend to value positive emotions over negative ones. Take happiness: there is a pervasive assumption in the U.S. that childhood is a naturally happy time and that children's happiness should be their parents' priority. In a recent survey, 73 percent of American parents rated happiness as the main goal in raising children, with Canada and France rating it even higher. In India only 49 percent of parents rated happiness so highly, while 51 percent prioritized achievement. Mexicans also valued success most, while Chinese parents ranked health first.

Yet this conviction about happiness, which seems self-evident to many of us, did not exist in the U.S. until the late 19th century, says George Mason University historian Peter Stearns. Before that time, 30 to 50 percent of children died before age five, and very young children were invariably put to work, sometimes at hard labor.

Our contemporary commitment to happiness has downsides, "for example, in measurably complicating reactions to childish unhappiness," Stearns says. As psychologists point out, negative feelings have important functions. Fear, for example, may feel bad, but it helps us avoid danger. A parent who's blissfully optimistic may be less vigilant about her toddler running into the street. Anger motivates us to confront those who threaten our goals or safety.

In fact, those convinced that negative feelings have their uses can exploit them. A classic study by psychologist Maya Tamir and her colleague, entitled "When Feeling Bad Is Expected to Be Good," illustrated this. In a laboratory experiment, the researchers showed that people who saw anger as helpful in a hostile negotiation–one that involved a landlord intent on getting overdue rent from a tenant–won more concessions in the bargaining if they revved up their anger beforehand.

Perhaps most crucially, our convictions about emotions–our own and others'–powerfully influence our closest relationships. In new research, University of Toronto psychology doctoral student

Angela M. Smith and their colleagues had subjects read a first-person narrative describing personal experiences with depression. The participants were then asked to imagine that this person was someone they knew and to pick from a list of potential likely responses to this classmate or neighbor. The study found that people who thought feelings were changeable felt more negatively about and less supportive of the depressed person.

Although the science of emotion beliefs in relationships is just starting, experts say we see these dynamics playing out every day. Many people are convinced that anger is toxic for relationships, Stanford's Gross says. A married person with this conviction might suppress their anger and not reveal important issues that, expressed in constructive ways, could improve their marriage. A parent who's angry with their child would likely also be upset with themselves and scared, Gross suggests. "So I then have just translated what would have been just anger into anger plus fear or sadness and upset. So that really complicates things," he adds.

We tend to think of our views of emotions as primarily psychological, but they also have significant social, cultural and historical dimensions, Stearns says, pointing to the recent field of "emotions history." Scientists are devoting new attention to how these ideas vary with country and shift over time. Consider gender: in our public discourse we often have heated debates about widespread views that anger is unbecoming in women and that vulnerability or sadness is so in men.

A study from 2019 sheds light on just where we are with these notions. A diverse group of young men and women read vignettes about a man or a woman crying in either stereotypically "masculine" settings such as firefighting and weightlifting or "feminine" settings such as nursing or figure skating. The participants approved much more of male firefighters weeping than male nurses. In the "masculine" settings, readers rated men shedding tears as more emotionally appropriate and strong.

The country we live in contributes to how we regard emotions and how we deal with them. In a study of nearly 4,000 people across

19 countries that is soon to be published in the journal *American Psychologist*, Tamir and her colleagues tested the relationship between using emotion regulation strategies with life satisfaction, depression and general psychological health.

In individualist countries such as Germany, the U.K. or the U.S., she explains, we think that emotions are inside us and tell us how we're doing. Yet research shows, Tamir says, that "in collectivist cultures, emotions are considered something that happens between people, and whether we feel inside good or bad doesn't really say anything about us. What is more important is how we behave and what we express." For example, presenting a poker face rather than showing feelings, she says, is harmful for people in individualist societies, but in more collectivist societies, people who do this actually feel better. This may be because in individualist societies, people value expressing authentic emotions, even unpleasant ones, she says. People in collectivist cultures value social harmony more, and expressing negative feelings can disrupt that.

As this research surges on many fronts, new insights such as these are constantly emerging. As Montclair State University psychologist Manuel Gonzalez says, the ways we think about emotion permeates our life; it is shaped by the way we are raised and later by work and even the national culture in the country where we live. "These beliefs permeate so heavily into how we deal with emotions," Gonzalez says, "how we handle our own emotions, what we allow ourselves to express [and] the ways that emotions pan out in our relationships—be it with family, with friends, at work, how we're perceived by other people and how they behave toward us."

About the Author

Francine Russo is a veteran journalist specializing in social sciences and relationships. She is author of Love after 50: How to Find It, Enjoy It, and Keep It *(Simon and Schuster, 2021).*

Being Empathetic Is Easier when Everyone's Doing It

By Elizabeth Svoboda

As a grid of video feeds blinks into view, attendees across the country prepare for an ideological collision. All have signed up for a virtual forum billed as an "empathy cafe," held to spark dialogue between police and community members. Among the participants are officers as well as people who've been burned in encounters with law enforcement.

The setup seems like a guaranteed powder keg. But as moderator Lou Zweier explains, this forum has some strict rules of engagement. "We're going to do four-minute speaking turns," he explains to the group, which will be separated into smaller breakout rooms. After one person in each breakout room gets a chance to speak about what's on their mind, someone else in the room—a person chosen as the "reflector"—will sum up the speaker's opinions and concerns as best they can, whether or not they agree. The reflector then becomes the next speaker and chooses a new reflector, and the process continues. "The listening and reflecting go around the circle," Zweier says. "Everyone gets a chance to speak and be heard."

This event, led by empathy educator Edwin Rutsch, offers a chance for minds to meet across the kind of yawning divide that's grown commonplace in the U.S. Such forums have popped up in part because trying to understand someone else's perspective doesn't always seem like a social bet that pays off.

Empathy is often defined as the capacity to understand what someone else is thinking and feeling. It is distinct from sympathy, which may imply pity (you might feel sympathy for someone in pain without grasping what they're going through), and from compassion, which involves a desire to ease someone's plight.

Because empathy can allow people to connect across political, racial and economic divides, it lays a foundation for acts of cooperation and caring that allow diverse societies to flourish. Higher levels of empathy are tied to both individual well-being and broader social cohesion.

When psychologist Sara Konrath set out to investigate empathy in the U.S., she found that it had been in decline for decades. She tracked Americans' self-reported empathy levels between 1979 and 2009 and found that people were increasingly less likely to agree with statements such as, "I sometimes try to understand my friends better by imagining how things look from their perspective."

Konrath's follow-up analysis, which tracked empathy levels between 1979 and 2018, did show rebounds in young people's willingness to take others' viewpoints and understand their feelings. But research highlights social and biological factors that continue to make empathy daunting. Polarization has been increasing, meaning that people see the world in fundamentally different ways and trust one another less. What's more, recent studies show that people shrink back from the mental effort it takes to understand what someone else is thinking and feeling. Meanwhile rates of loneliness, resentment and depression in the U.S. are high.

To promote empathy as a collective good, researchers have rolled out a smorgasbord of education programs. There are classroom programs for elementary schoolers, training seminars for employees and even immersive empathy retreats. New research shows that empathy instruction can boost people's ability to engage reflectively across political divides. Yet fully grasping someone else's experience is a heavy cognitive lift.

Increasing empathy, says Stanford University social psychologist Jamil Zaki, will take more than teaching skills such as listening actively to others. Empathy is a socially motivated process, Zaki and other researchers say, meaning that people won't necessarily empathize just because they know how. Instead–much as kids with athletic peers often want to excel at sports–people want to understand others when they enter into communities where empathy is the established norm.

Neuroscientists are beginning to piece together a clearer picture of empathy's neural origins. When researchers elicit empathy by, say, showing people a film clip about what someone else is going through, a series of interconnected brain regions activate on functional MRI scans. Among these regions are the dorsomedial prefrontal cortex, which helps to gauge other people's emotional states, and the anterior insula, which is involved in processing pain. Similarly, researchers have identified single neurons in the dorsomedial prefrontal cortex that encode information about others' thoughts.

Our ability to perceive other people's inner states most likely evolved because it helps to forge the kinds of strong social ties that promote survival. In human ancestral environments, nomadic groups understood one another's emotions and state of mind; the bonds among them deepened, helping the group to function as a resilient unit.

Whereas empathy has long been an adaptive way of ensuring social cohesion, it also exacts a steep cognitive price. Taking someone else's perspective is a complex, challenging operation for the brain, in part because it requires a sophisticated assessment of what the other person may be thinking and feeling. In one 2020 study at the University of Liverpool in England, researchers found that empathy for others' pain requires a host of different brain networks to interact, including some responsible for inferring others' mental state. (When people perceive their own pain, on the other hand, their brain activity related to understanding others diminishes.)

A series of experiments led by Pennsylvania State University psychologist C. Daryl Cameron found that most individuals prefer to opt out of the cognitive effort empathy requires, especially if they don't know the other person well. In multiple rounds of game play, Cameron offered participants in a study two card games to choose from: an "objective deck" game, which asked them to describe the appearance of people on the cards, or an "empathy deck" game, which asked them to describe the people's possible experiences and feelings based on their expressions. Most people stated that they preferred the objective deck.

In part, that's because it's harder to empathize with someone who feels distant or unknown than with a close loved one. "The more shared experiences you have with someone, the more of a rich, nuanced representation you can draw on," Cameron says. But empathy for someone whose experience feels alien–the person who disagrees with you online, the man in a tent outside the subway or even a cousin who spouts extremist views–is a different matter. A host of disquieting unknowns arises: Is identifying with this person going to put you in danger? Will it compel you to sacrifice something important, such as time, money, tranquility?

When such anticipated costs overwhelm people, they're more prone to withdraw altogether rather than trying to understand where the other person is coming from. "We are quite adept at learning how to manage our emotional environments to cultivate what we want to feel," Cameron says. "Empathizing with a stranger, taking on their experiences–either negative or positive experiences–people find it difficult, they find it costly. And the more they feel that way, the less they opt in." In a 2020 study at the University of Lübeck in Germany, fMRI scans of people who'd just heard stories about mass tragedies showed less activation in their brains' core empathy networks compared with those who had not heard the disturbing stories.

But larger structural forces are likely at play, too. Wealth inequality in the U.S. has steadily risen since the 1980s, and people in rarefied income brackets often have little motivation to understand the struggles of those at the poverty line. "We're much more segregated economically nowadays," Konrath says. "That can impair our ability to see and to care and to have those people be our neighbors and friends that we naturally want to help."

The impulse to sidestep empathy's complications also leads people into polarized online echo chambers–many of which also persist in the physical world–where we're less and less likely to maintain friendships with those whose views differ from our own. It's easier than ever to be a water strider, gliding away from others with frictionless ease.

That suspicion and detachment are what Rutsch, a former computer systems administrator turned empathy educator, aims to dissolve through empathy cafes and other similar events. He founded the Center for Building a Culture of Empathy in 2010, with an aim to create a headquarters for the global empathy movement. Rutsch based his approach on that of humanistic psychologist Carl Rogers, who used reflective listening techniques to build trust and rapport with clients.

Rutsch has traveled around the country with pop-up "empathy tents," which he pitches near demonstrations and protests. Once he pitched a tent just beyond a 1,000-person rally in Los Angeles for former president Donald Trump, which was also attended by large numbers of counterprotesters. Rutsch invited in six people from each side. Then he mediated six pairs in listening carefully to one another, then stating their own understanding of the other person's thinking. "Of those six pairs, five of them ended up giving each other hugs afterward," Rutsch says. "On the other side of the street, they were screaming and yelling at each other, and the police were having to keep them apart."

Rutsch attributes such outcomes to the intentional structure of these chats. Even if the other person says a false or off-the-wall statement–for example, that the 2020 election was stolen–"you reflect back your understanding of what they have said," he says. "When it is your turn to speak, you can challenge what they have said. They have to take it into their consciousness to be able to reflect it. That means they have to listen to you. They cannot live just in their own worldview."

In these dialogues, listening and being carefully listened to in return often begins to soften conspiracists' armor. "Knowing that you were willing to listen to them, they often drop their judgments after a while and get more real," Rutsch says. "You get to a deeper understanding of each other and see each other's humanity. You may get to a deeper fear, perhaps, that is the reason for the lie."

Many researchers have devised programs that similarly help participants hone specific empathy skills. Some, for adults, focus on how to empathize in work interactions; others, for elementary-aged students, teach the nuts and bolts of how to take another person's perspective.

In Roots of Empathy, now offered in hundreds of schools across the U.S. and around the world, a local family brings their young baby into the classroom once a month, and trained instructors guide students to practice "perspective taking" by identifying what the baby might be thinking and feeling at different times. In studies, elementary schoolers enrolled in Roots of Empathy were better than control students at understanding others' emotions. They also proved more likely to help others in the classroom by the end of the school year, based on reports from their peers.

Yet established empathy programs such as these often rest on the assumption that once people have empathetic skills in their arsenal, they'll be more apt to put them to use. That's not always the case, says Harvard social psychologist Erika Weisz. Studies show that even when people know how to empathize intellectually, they may not exercise that ability unless they truly feel the desire to do so. If they expect empathy to be costly or unpleasant, for instance, some people will refrain from it no matter their training or skill level.

Like Zaki and Cameron, Weisz frames empathy as a socially motivated process–one that's dependent not just on what someone knows about empathy but on how compelled they feel to show it. She's found that another way to nudge people toward empathy–and keep them there–is to embed them in communities where empathy is a baseline expectation. "People want to increase their empathy if you tell them, essentially, it will help them socially," Weisz says. "That is a perfectly reasonable leverage." Unlike empathy skills training, which teaches specific methods of relating to others, Weisz's approach involves building communities that value and reward empathetic behavior. It draws on a kind of constructive peer pressure.

In a pilot program at four California middle schools, Weisz tracked the effects of establishing empathy as a social norm among students. She held three virtual workshops where seventh graders completed activities such as reading stories their classmates wrote about why empathy was important to them. Several weeks after the workshops, students in the program's social-norm group proved more motivated to show empathy toward others.

Weisz attributes these results to the relative ease and simplicity of following a social norm—as opposed to, say, practicing a just-learned empathy skill every day. "My enthusiasm about motivated empathy interventions comes from the fact that they complement people's existing daily lives," Weisz says. "You don't need to completely add a new variable. It's just like riding a wave that's already cresting."

This approach informs the empathy program at Third Street Elementary School in Los Angeles, which I visited last spring. Drawing on a curriculum from Harvard's Caring Schools Network (CSN), Third Street teaches students empathetic skills—and crucially, the students learn to exercise those skills within a community that models empathy at every level. "Character education programs are in a sense about literacy, that kids know right from wrong," says CSN psychologist Rick Weissbourd. "We're more focused on identity or moral motivation: What makes someone want to be a good person in the world, or what motivates someone to care for other people?"

During a perspective-taking exercise, Laura, a parent volunteer in one of Third Street's fourth-grade classrooms, asked students: "What would you do if you saw a student tease another student because of what they're eating?" The kids then sorted themselves into groups around the room based on how they'd answer: ask an adult for help, ignore the situation, tell the unkind kid to stop, or check in with the person who was teased.

"The person who teases the other person might keep doing it," said one boy, arguing for telling the offender to stop.

Not everyone agreed. "It really honestly depends on who it is," one girl says. "If it was my friend, I would probably go over there." If it's not her friend, she added, she would just get out of the way.

"You don't want to make it a bigger problem than it already is," another girl adds.

As each student chimed in, the rest listened attentively, taking in the conflicting opinions. Through this kind of habitual, focused listening, Weissbourd explains, students learn to better appreciate where others are coming from. And it's not just adults leading this dynamic. If a student is having a beef with someone else, they can approach any kid on campus wearing an orange hat. These peer counselors will listen carefully to their concerns and help them solve the problem.

In surveys at U.S. schools, students who participate in CSN curricula report being more helpful than control-group students, and their listening and perspective-taking skills improve. Third Street is a cocoon of sorts, a chance for kids to marinate in empathetic community. That could help prepare them for more challenging encounters later on, to cultivate empathy for those with whom they disagree profoundly.

"The kind of empathy we see in everyday life, a lot of it is you embedding empathy within valuable social relationships," Cameron says. "One approach might be to think about using that relational value as a starting point and then going to the harder places—extending that out to someone you don't know or even someone who's an enemy."

Socially modeling empathy affects not just how community members behave but the way their brains work, says neuroscientist Grit Hein of Germany's University Hospital Würzburg. In a 2024 study, Hein's adult subjects watched videos of people getting hit with an intense burst of air and reacting in pain. People who watched a person respond empathically to the blast videos were likely to follow suit, whereas those who watched another person shrug off the videos acted equally blasé.

Hein found that people who witnessed an empathetic reaction were more likely to rate the recipient's pain as high, whereas those who saw the low-empathy video rated the pain as low. Those who saw the social example of concern also had more activity in their brain's anterior insula, which governs empathy processing, than people who saw the indifferent example.

"If you're surrounded by empathic individuals, it really has an influence. It increases how your brain responds to the pain of another person," Hein says. "The bad news is, it also works the other way around." In other words, if you're surrounded by people who are indifferent or hostile, you're apt to mirror their social example as well. One 2023 study shows that people who identify as politically liberal have stronger empathetic brain activation than conservatives, raising questions about whether social norms within each political group might drive empathy differences between them.

Compared with Third Street students, attendees at Rutsch's online cafe are scattered across the country and navigating political divides. The forum's clear rules of engagement, however, create their own kind of fast-forwarded cultural norm. Only one person speaks at a time; the "reflector" must refrain from passing judgment; each person gets to choose their own fresh topic to discuss.

At first, the tension within the group is palpable. A community member named Sushila says she wants to know why police always dress like they're going into battle. "If I were to see them in riot gear or carrying batons, that would make me very uncomfortable," she says.

After Sushila speaks, Roger, now a lead official at Oakland's Community Police Review Agency, tries to "reflect" what she's saying. "You recognize that how you see them, specifically what you see them wearing, can potentially change that relationship," he says. "You see the militarization as calling for a conversation, for the police to engage the community and explain why they see the equipment that they have as being necessary."

What's interesting about the discussions isn't so much the reflectors' input, which mostly mirrors what the speakers say. It's how, over time, being intensively listened to—and intensively listening in return—seems to influence which new topics each speaker elects to bring up.

As the conversation continues, the participants' stances shift toward curiosity—and even optimism. Sushila talks about planning events to help cops and community members establish a better relationship. She then recalls a time when a sheriff in her city encouraged this kind of rapport by acting in *The Vagina Monologues*.

Sushila explains what that meant to her: "The fact that a police authority could show vulnerability and be so real ... I think she's doing a great public service."

For the remainder of the chat, people's contributions center on how to forge relationships that benefit both police and community members—and how to keep confrontations between them from spiraling. "We need to get more law-enforcement officers to these events," a security officer named John says toward the end, stressing that further similar exchanges could be valuable in bringing people together.

This dynamic parallels what political scientists Joshua Kalla of Yale University and David Broockman of the University of California, Berkeley, found in studies of more than 6,000 U.S. voters who chatted with canvassers about politicized topics, such as immigration and transgender rights. When canvassers engaged voters in typical back-and-forth arguments, few voters who had prejudicial opinions changed them. But when canvassers showed interest in understanding voters and asked them to share their perspectives, voters' prejudiced views diminished for at least four months following the conversation. Likewise, Stanford psychologist Luiza A. Santos and her colleagues found that when people saw empathy as an asset in communicating with political opponents, they used more conciliatory language, and opponents were more likely to see their messages as persuasive.

The norms of polarized times, though, discourage such nuanced exchanges. Takedowns of opposing views get praised in activist circles and upvoted on social media, and civilly engaging with the other side can feel perilously close to endorsing harmful beliefs. But Kalla and Broockman's research, as well as Rutsch's forums, makes a surprising case for more empathetic, reflective social engagement: it's being thoroughly heard, not condemned, that entices people to reject bigotry.

This style of listening, Rutsch emphasizes, does not mean absorbing others' stances as your own. This kind of spongelike empathy is what Yale psychologist Paul Bloom rejects in his 2016 book *Against Empathy*.

When you take on someone else's feelings, Bloom argues, those feelings rub off on you in ways that can interfere with logical decision-making–and even with helping. He also notes that too much empathy can be exhausting, draining people's emotional resources in ways that put them off engaging with others. (Frontline health-care workers and others who witness trauma at close range may be especially vulnerable to this kind of fatigue.)

Bloom's critics say empathy can coexist with this kind of deliberative reasoning–and doesn't (or shouldn't) involve identification with others to the point of exhaustion. Empathizing constructively means "sensing into the felt experience of someone else," Rutsch says, "but it's not like you're taking it on to the point where you stop being present with them. It's just about showing that you hear and understand the other person." That understanding, in turn, can actually motivate the informed helping behavior Bloom calls for.

Cognitive science research helps to explain how such virtuous empathetic cycles can pick up speed. When people feel heard and understood, they tend to feel safer, and nervous system fight-or-flight responses recede, allowing them to better process what others are saying. A sense of safety may also help relieve the feeling of being overwhelmed and social angst that fuel the antiempathy bias Cameron describes.

Over time, reflective one-on-one dynamics feed into a broader environment where empathy starts to feel like its own reward. People grow compelled to understand one another in communities that model the practice–whether they're groups of three or four, as in Rutsch's online sessions, or entire workplaces and schools. Weisz hopes researchers can secure funding for future studies of how well social norm tweaks motivate empathy in settings like schools and workplaces.

After the empathy cafe breakout groups merge back into one, some attendees reflect on how to ease people into a practice that can feel, at first, like leaping into the abyss. "I think it'd be really valuable to do this as the first step in a longer process," says a community member named Daniel. "Once you get used to hearing other people and knowing what different opinions are, knowing what different approaches are, then you can get to work on other things."

About the Author

Elizabeth Svoboda is a science writer in San Jose, Calif., and author of, most recently, The Life Heroic: How to Unleash Your Most Amazing Self *(Zest, 2019).*

Facial Expressions Do Not Reveal Emotions

By Lisa Feldman Barrett

Do your facial movements broadcast your emotions to other people? If you think the answer is yes, think again. This question is under contentious debate. Some experts maintain that people around the world make specific, recognizable faces that express certain emotions, such as smiling in happiness, scowling in anger and gasping with widened eyes in fear. They point to hundreds of studies that appear to demonstrate that smiles, frowns, and so on are universal facial expressions of emotion. They also often cite Charles Darwin's 1872 book *The Expression of the Emotions in Man and Animals* to support the claim that universal expressions evolved by natural selection.

Other scientists point to a mountain of counter evidence showing that facial movements during emotions vary too widely to be universal beacons of emotional meaning. People may smile in hatred when plotting their enemy's downfall and scowl in delight when they hear a bad pun. In Melanesian culture, a wide-eyed gasping face is a symbol of aggression, not fear. These experts say the alleged universal expressions just represent cultural stereotypes. To be clear, both sides in the debate acknowledge that facial movements vary for a given emotion; the disagreement is about whether there is enough uniformity to detect what someone is feeling.

This debate is not just academic; the outcome has serious consequences. Today you can be turned down for a job because a so-called emotion-reading system watching you on camera applied artificial intelligence to evaluate your facial movements unfavorably during an interview. In a U.S. court of law, a judge or jury may sometimes hand down a harsher sentence, even death, if they think a defendant's face showed a lack of remorse. Children in preschools across the country are taught to recognize smiles as happiness, scowls as anger and other expressive stereotypes from books, games and posters of disembodied faces. And for children on the autism spectrum, some of whom have difficulty perceiving emotion in others, these teachings do not translate to better communication.

So who is right? The answer involves an unwitting physician, a scientific error and a century-long misinterpretation of Darwin's writing. Ironically, his own observations offer a powerful resolution that is transforming the modern understanding of emotion.

The assumption of universal facial expressions can be traced back to several sources, most notably a set of photographs by 19th-century French physician Guillaume-Benjamin-Amand Duchenne. In the early days of photography, Duchenne electrically stimulated people's facial muscles and photographed the contractions.

His photographs inspired Darwin to propose in *Expression* that certain facial movements were universal signs of emotion. In happiness, Darwin wrote, people smile. In sadness, they frown. The way the story is usually told, Darwin discovered that emotions have innate, biologically based expressions that are made and recognized universally and shared with other animals. That story presents facial movements as a sort of signaling system in which you can look at a person's face, detect their emotional state and receive important information to keep you—and them—alive and healthy.

Or so it would seem. A preponderance of evidence shows that Darwin was wrong, and his mistake was a doozy. In real life, people express a given emotion with tremendous variability. In anger, for example, people in urban cultures scowl (or make some of the facial movements for a scowl) only about 35 percent of the time, according to meta-analyses of studies measuring facial movement during emotion. Scowls are also not specific to anger because people scowl for other reasons, such as when they are concentrating or when they have gas. The same tremendous variation occurs for every emotion studied—and for every other measure that purportedly tells us about someone's emotional state, whether it's their physiology, voice or brain activity.

Emotion AI systems, therefore, do not detect emotions. They detect physical signals, such as facial muscle movements, not the psychological meaning of those signals. The conflation of movement and meaning is deeply embedded in Western culture and in science. An example is a recent high-profile study that applied machine learning to more than six million internet videos of faces. The human raters, who trained the AI system, were asked to label facial movements in the videos, but the only labels they were given to use were emotion words, such as "angry," rather than physical descriptions, such as "scowling." Moreover there was no objective way to confirm what, if anything, the anonymous people in the videos were feeling in those moments.

There's also considerable evidence that facial movements are just one signal of many in a much larger array of contextual information that our brain takes in. Show people a grimacing face in isolation, and they may perceive pain or frustration. But show the identical face on a runner crossing the finish line of a race, and the same grimace conveys triumph. The face is often a weaker signal of a person's internal state than other signals in the array.

Darwin's *Expression* suggests that instances of a particular emotion, such as anger, share a distinct, immutable, physical cause or state–an essence–that makes the instances similar even if they have superficial differences. Scientists have proposed a variety of essences, some of which are easily seen, such as facial movements, and others, such as complex, intertwined patterns of heart rate, breathing and body temperature, that are observed only with specialized instruments. This belief in essences, called essentialism, is compellingly intuitive. It's also pernicious because it is virtually impossible to prove that an essence doesn't exist. People who believe in essences but fail to observe them despite repeated attempts often continue to believe in them anyway. Researchers, in particular, tend to justify their belief by suggesting that tools and methods are not yet sufficient to locate the essences they seek.

A solution to this conundrum can be found in Darwin's more famous book *On the Origin of Species*, written 13 years before *Expression*. Ironically, it is celebrated for helping biology "escape the paralyzing grip of essentialism," according to heralded biologist

Ernst Mayr. Before *Origin* was published, scholars believed that each biological species had an ideal form, created by God, with defining properties–essences–that distinguished it from all other species. Think of this as the "dog show" version of biology. In a dog show, each competitor is judged against a hypothetical ideal dog. Deviation from the ideal is considered error. Darwin's *Origin* proposed, radically, that a species is a vast population of varied individuals with no essence at its core. The ideal dog doesn't exist–it is a statistical summary of many diverse dogs. Variation is not error; it is a necessary ingredient for natural selection by the environment. When it came to emotions, however, Darwin fell prey to essentialism, ignoring his most important discovery.

The power of essentialism led Darwin to some beautifully ridiculous ideas about emotion, including that emotional imbalance can cause frizzy hair and that insects express fear and anger by frantically rubbing their body parts together.

Essentialism likewise appears to lure designers of emotion AI systems to follow Darwin down this comfortable path, with its assumption that emotions evolved via natural selection to serve important functions. But if you actually read *Expression*, you'll find that Darwin barely mentioned natural selection. He also did not write that facial expressions are functional products of evolution. In fact, he wrote the opposite: that smiles, frowns, eye widening and other physical expressions were "purposeless"–vestigial movements that no longer serve a function. He made this statement more than 10 times in *Expression*. For Darwin, emotional expressions were compelling evidence that humans are animals and that we've evolved. By his logic, if we share expressions with other animals, but the expressions are functionally useless for us, they must have come from a long-gone, common ancestor for whom the expressions were useful.

Expression has been cited incorrectly for more than 100 years. How did this happen? I discovered the answer lurking in the work of an early-20th-century psychologist, Floyd Allport. In his 1924 book *Social Psychology*, Allport made a sweeping inference from Darwin's writing to say that expressions begin as vestigial in newborns but quickly assume useful social functions. He wrote, "Instead of the biologically useful reaction being present in the ancestor and the expressive vestige in the descendant, we regard both these functions as present in the descendant, the former serving as a basis from which the latter develops."

Allport's idea, though incorrect, was attributed back to Darwin and eagerly adopted by like-minded scientists. They could now write about facial expressions as universal and claim to be the heirs of the unassailable Charles Darwin. With a single sentence, Allport misdirected the Western understanding of emotions, not only in science but in law, medicine, the eyes of the public and now emotion AI systems.

Nevertheless, this scientific tale has a happy ending because there is a name for the kind of variation we observe in real-life instances of emotion. It's the same variation that Darwin himself observed in animal species. In *Origin*, Darwin described an animal species as a collection of varied individuals with no biological essence at its core. This key observation became known more generally as population thinking, and it's supported by the modern study of genetics.

Population thinking has been revolutionizing biology for the past century, and it is now revolutionizing the science of emotion. Like a species, a given emotion such as fear, grief or elation is a vast population of varied instances. People may indeed widen their eyes and gasp in fear, but they may also scowl in fear, cry in fear, laugh in the face of fear and, in some cultures, even fall asleep in fear. There is no essence. Variation is the norm, and it is intimately linked to a person's physiology and situation, just as variation in a species is linked to the environment its members live in.

An increasing number of emotion researchers are taking population thinking more seriously and moving beyond the essentialist ideas of the past. It is time for emotion AI proponents and the companies that make and market these products to cut the hype and acknowledge that facial muscle movements do not map universally to specific emotions. The evidence is clear that the same emotion can accompany different facial movements and that the same facial movements can have different (or no) emotional meaning. Variety, not uniformity, is the rule.

Darwin's *Expression* is best viewed as a historical text, not a definitive scientific guide. That leads to a deeper lesson here: Science is not truth by authority. Science is the quantification of doubt by repeated observation in varied contexts. Even the most exceptional scientists can be wrong. Fortunately, mistakes are part of the scientific process. They are opportunities for discovery.

This is an opinion and analysis article, and the views expressed by the author or authors are not necessarily those of Scientific American.

About the Author

Lisa Feldman Barrett is a professor of psychology at Northeastern University. She is the author of several books, including How Emotions Are Made: The Secret Life of the Brain. *Follow her on Twitter @LFeldmanBarrett.*

Too Much Emotional Intelligence Is a Bad Thing

By Agata Blaszczak-Boxe

Recognizing when a friend or colleague feels sad, angry or surprised is key to getting along with others. But a new study suggests that a knack for eavesdropping on feelings may sometimes come with an extra dose of stress. This and other research challenge the prevailing view that emotional intelligence is uniformly beneficial to its bearer.

In a study published in the September 2016 issue of *Emotion*, psychologists Myriam Bechtoldt and Vanessa Schneider of the Frankfurt School of Finance and Management in Germany asked 166 male university students a series of questions to measure their emotional smarts. For example, they showed the students photographs of people's faces and asked them to what extent feelings such as happiness or disgust were being expressed. The students then had to give job talks in front of judges displaying stern facial expressions. The scientists measured concentrations of the stress hormone cortisol in the students' saliva before and after the talk.

In students who were rated more emotionally intelligent, the stress measures increased more during the experiment and took longer to go back to baseline. The findings suggest that some people may be too emotionally astute for their own good, says Hillary Anger Elfenbein, a professor of organizational behavior at Washington University in St. Louis, who was not involved in the study. "Sometimes you can be so good at something that it causes trouble," she notes.

Indeed, the study adds to previous research hinting at a dark side of emotional intelligence. A study published in 2002 in *Personality and Individual Differences* suggested that emotionally perceptive people might be particularly susceptible to feelings of depression and hopelessness. Furthermore, several studies, including one published in 2013 in *PLOS ONE*, have implied that emotional intelligence can be used to manipulate others for personal gain.

More research is needed to see how exactly the relation between emotional intelligence and stress would play out in women and in people of different ages and education levels. Nevertheless, emotional intelligence is a useful skill to have, as long as you learn to also properly cope with emotions–both others' and your own, says Bechtoldt, a professor of organizational behavior. For example, some sensitive individuals may assume responsibility for other people's sadness or anger, which ultimately stresses them out. Remember, Bechtoldt says, "you are not responsible for how other people feel."

Can You Tell Someone's Emotional State from an MRI?

By Veronique Greenwood

A number of studies have used functional MRI to see what our brain looks like as we recall pleasant memories, watch scary movies or listen to sad music. Scientists have even had some success telling which of these stimuli a subject is experiencing by looking at his or her scans. But does this mean it is possible to tell what emotions we are experiencing in the absence of prompts, as we let our mind wander naturally? That is a difficult question to answer, in part because psychologists disagree about how emotions should be defined. Nevertheless, some scientists are trying to tackle it.

In a study reported in the June 2016 issue of *Cerebral Cortex*, Heini Saarimäki of Aalto University in Finland and her colleagues observed volunteers in a brain scanner who were being prompted to recall memories they associated with words drawn from six emotional categories or to reflect on a movie clip selected to provoke certain emotions. The participants also completed a questionnaire about how closely linked different emotions were–rating, for instance, whether "anxiety" is closer to "fear" than to "happiness." The researchers found that pattern-recognition software could detect which category of emotion a person had been prompted with. In addition, the more closely he or she linked words in the questionnaire, the more his or her brain scans for those emotions resembled one another.

Another study, published in September 2016 in *PLOS Biology* by Kevin LaBar of Duke University and his colleagues, attempted to match brain scans of people lying idle in a scanner to seven predefined patterns associated with specific emotions provoked in an earlier study. The researchers found they could predict the subjects' self-reported emotions from the scans about 75 percent of the time.

Not everyone agrees, however, that studying emotions this way–as averages of many people's brains while they undergo a stimulus—makes sense. Psychology professor Lisa Feldman Barrett of Northeastern University and author of *How Emotions Are Made* (Houghton Mifflin Harcourt, 2017), who was not involved in either study, says that so far no one has clearly demonstrated that patterns taken from one study can be used to recognize the same emotion in another group of people provoked by a different stimulus. Such brain patterns, Barrett says, are just statistical summaries, not unique signatures that exist only when someone has a certain experience. And one person's emotions may not look the same in a brain scan as another person's. "Maybe you have five [different] patterns for anger, maybe I have seven, maybe somebody else has two," Barrett adds. "Maybe they overlap, maybe they don't."

Going forward, we are likely to see diverse perspectives on what emotion is and how to study it. "For now," Saarimäki says wryly, "I think we are still safer if you just ask people how they are feeling, rather than trying to read their brain."

About the Author

Veronique Greenwood is a science writer and essayist whose work has appeared in the New York Times, *the* Atlantic *and* National Geographic, *among others.*

You Can Literally Sniff Out Other People's Inner Feelings

By Marta Zaraska

After a viral infection robbed Chrissi Kelly, an American archeologist living in the U.K., of her sense of smell, she no longer felt like herself. It was as if she were "floating away," untethered from the rest of the world. Smell, she says, is something that binds us to nature and to our family, and without it, we cannot fully participate in everyday life. She missed the social part of scents: the deep joy of hugging a loved one and taking in their personal aroma. "I found living without the sense of smell profoundly disorienting," she says.

Kelly felt so strongly about what happened to her that she started a charity called AbScent to help people with smell loss. Kelly's perception that smell forms part of a person's identity is now receiving confirmation from recent research findings. A 2023 study from European researchers found, for instance, that not only can we pick up the scent of other people's fear or anxiety, but such emotions affect how we feel, too. Another study from China showed that people with better olfaction have more friends. "We see all kinds of behavioral effects," says Shani Agron, a neurobiologist at the Weizmann Institute of Science in Israel.

Humans have a long history of disregarding our noses—even Darwin claimed that the sense of smell is of "extremely slight service" to people. According to Bettina Pause, a biological psychologist at Heinrich Heine University Düsseldorf in Germany, one reason may be that social olfaction happens outside of our conscious attention. "The only thing I might know about this conversation is that my body feeling changes," she says. Yet humans seem quite able to pick out someone else's body odor. One study found that after shaking hands with people of the same gender, people reflexively sniffed their right hand more than twice as often as they did before the greeting.

We pick up quite a lot of information from sniffing the body odor of people around us: we can recognize our kin, tell who is genetically related and pinpoint potential friends (we tend to choose friends who are genetically similar to us and have similar body odor). In one study, most new mothers were able to identify their baby by its smell after spending as little as 10 minutes together, and newborns can recognize their mother, too.

Adult human sniffers, meanwhile, can match pairs of identical twins by their body odor, even if the siblings live apart. In a 2022 study, researchers at the Weizmann Institute of Science managed to predict which volunteers would bond together simply by comparing their body odor—a task performed both by human smellers and an electronic nose (a device that looks like an old CB radio with a hose). The scientists discovered that people who smelled similar to each other were more likely to enjoy chatting and report that they felt instant chemistry. This goes along with earlier research showing that we subconsciously choose friends who share some of the same genes.

What's more, if we were to chat with someone feeling happy, chances are we would detect their current emotional state through smells that reach the nose. In one experiment conducted in the Netherlands, volunteers watched cheerful videos while holding absorbent pads in their armpits. Later, when another group sniffed the pads, measurements of their facial muscles' activity revealed that their mood improved, too: their smile muscles moved more.

Yet it's not only happy feelings that can be communicated through body odor. A 2020 study by Pause and colleagues showed that women's brains reacted more strongly when they smelled the sweat of men who had played an aggressively competitive game compared with the odors of men who had just enjoyed a calm construction game. It turns out that women also proved to be particularly sensitive to odors that signaled male anxiety. On picking up such odors, they became more risk-avoidant and less trusting. "Anxiety is a signal of, 'Please, I need help,'" Pause says. This, she believes, may explain why women appear more attuned to the smell of anxiety–historically, in distressing situations, it was women that cared for the young and the feeble. Such evolutionary links could also explain why women with more discerning noses perform better at tests of empathy, as revealed in a small 2022 study carried out by Pause and her colleagues.

In general, a sensitive nose seems to be an asset that enhances our deeply social life. Those who could better tell apart everyday odors also reported less loneliness, a 2020 study of 221 volunteers concluded. In other experiments, people with a better sense of smell had a larger social network and more friends, and they met with those friends more often. Functional magnetic resonance imaging of the brain, meanwhile, revealed that the same brain circuits may be involved in both our sense of smell and the size of our social circle.

For now, however, the mechanisms of how exactly humans pick up body odors and translate them into changes in our behaviors remain largely a mystery. "It's a multifaceted problem that we have yet to really begin to tease apart," says Johan Lundström, a neuroscientist at the Karolinska Institute in Sweden. Scientists are also just beginning to pinpoint which chemicals in body odor may be responsible for influencing social connections. One such molecule may be hexanal, which gives off a pleasant whiff of freshly cut grass–and appears to boost trust in people. Yet we still don't know if those who have more hexanal in their body odor are perceived as more trustworthy, says Monique Smeets, a social psychologist at Utrecht University in the Netherlands.

More research will likely follow because, as Agron says, "The pandemic really put a spotlight on the sense of smell." Even though Omicron appears to be less damaging to our noses than previous COVID variants were, a 2023 study estimated that 11.7 percent of adults of European ancestry who have been infected with Omicron have had some amount of olfactory dysfunction. People with smell loss may end up missing out on important but subconscious ways of communicating with others. And smell should be valued because olfaction is the most honest of our senses–something that, unlike our words or facial expressions, we just can't fake. "I can laugh even though I'm sad or aggressive, but I cannot intentionally change my chemical messages," Pause says. "It's kind of the only information which you can trust."

About the Author

Marta Zaraska is a freelance writer based in France and author of Growing Young: How Friendship, Optimism and Kindness Can Help You Live to 100 *(Appetite by Random House, 2020). She wrote "Shrinking Animals" in the June 2018 issue of* Scientific American.

Sniffing Women's Tears Makes Men Less Aggressive

By Rachel Nuwer

When someone starts to cry, other people oftentimes feel empathy and concern. But the biological reasons for shedding tears can extend beyond merely prompting a sense of compassion. The tears themselves appear to take on a role as a chemical peacemaker between men and women, new research has discovered.

Women's tears act to reduce aggression in men who are close enough to catch a whiff of the waterworks, according to findings published in *PLOS Biology* and confirmed through human behavioral studies, brain imaging and molecular biology. The researchers speculate that tears from people who aren't women likely have a similar effect, but this has yet to be tested.

The new paper suggests that a fundamental reason why women shed emotional tears is "to convey a chemical signal that lowers aggression," says Shani Agron, co-lead author of the study, which she conducted for her doctoral degree in neurobiology at the Weizmann Institute of Science in Israel. (Agron has since graduated.) "We believe this is a shared mechanism of many mammals."

Producing tears has long been considered a uniquely human behavior, but that's a flawed notion, says co-senior author Noam Sobel, a neurobiologist at the Weizmann Institute of Science, who was Agron's adviser. Dogs, for example, shed tears when they reunite with their owners after a period of separation. Baby mouse tears contain molecular cues that sway female mice to reject male advances, while pheromones in female mouse tears encourage males to stop fighting each other and mate with the female instead. Mole rat subordinates, moreover, go so far as to cover themselves in their own tears to chemically deflect aggression from dominant members in their group.

Humans, like other mammals, communicate information with body odors. But it wasn't obvious that tears would have any olfactory effect on human behavior because people cannot perceive a smell from them. Additionally, while most mammals have a second olfactory organ that is responsible for detecting pheromones, in humans, this organ is thought to be vestigial.

The first evidence that tears can chemically influence human behavior emerged in 2011, when Sobel and his colleagues published a study in *Science* that showed that women's tears reduced levels of testosterone and self-reported sexual arousal in men. This earlier work raised more questions than it provided answers for. It took years of effort to conduct a more thorough follow-up, in part because of the difficulty of collecting tears from donors. The researchers need at least one milliliter of tears to use on each experimental participant, which is "a *lot* of tears," Sobel says. Using an onion or other irritant to force someone's eyes to water is not an option, Agron adds, because "these are a completely different type of tears."

To collect the tears used in the new study, the team put out a call for volunteers who cry easily. Only a few men showed up, and none was able to produce enough tears to qualify. Of the 100 or so women who volunteered, only six were able to supply sufficient amounts of tears to warrant collection. Participants could use any means they wanted to elicit the tears—from listening to sad music to reading a sad letter—but most turned to the lab's expansive "library of sad movies," Agron says. In addition to tears, the researchers also collected drops of saline solution that they trickled down women's face for use in control experiments.

The researchers next gathered data from 25 male volunteers who played a game in the lab that is often used in studies of aggression. During the competitive game, participants were led to believe that their opponent was another person. It was in fact a computer algorithm, however. Occasionally, the opponent stole money from the participants, who could then either choose to take revenge, with no monetary gain for themselves, or let their opponent get away with it but continue collecting more money for themselves. The researchers calculated aggressiveness by the number of times a participant chose revenge divided by the number of times they were provoked. The team also repeated this experiment in a second group of 26 male volunteers who played the game while inside a magnetic resonance imaging scanner, allowing their brain activity data to be collected.

All participants played the game twice, and before each session, they were asked to inhale from a "sniff jar" that they were told contained "assorted odors" but that in fact held either tears or saline. The researchers found that when the men sniffed the women's tears, they were nearly 44 percent less aggressive in the game than when they sniffed the saline solution. The behavioral reduction in aggression was also accompanied by neuronal changes. The researchers observed that the men's brain post-tear sniff exhibited less activity in the prefrontal cortex and the left anterior insula, regions that are associated with aggression and decision-making. Connectivity between the anterior insula and amygdala, a region that is responsible for emotional processing and also part of the olfactory network, increased as well.

Working with colleagues at Duke University, the team used molecular biology methods to test the effects of tears and saline on 62 human olfactory receptors in a lab dish. They identified four receptors that responded to tears but not saline. This finding helps to answer "a major question" about how pheromonelike signals are processed in humans, Agron says.

Agron, Sobel and their colleagues are now interested in running future experiments to test the effect of women's tears on other women and that of babies' tears on adults. Sobel hypothesizes that baby tears, especially, will likely have an aggressiveness-lowering effect on adults. "Babies cannot communicate with you in language," he says. "But evolution may have provided babies with this tool to lower aggression."

The fact that people continue to be able to produce tears throughout adulthood, Agron adds, indicates that crying is probably "a behavior that serves us throughout life."

About the Author

Rachel Nuwer is a science journalist and author. Her latest book is I Feel Love: MDMA and the Quest for Connection in a Fractured World *(Bloomsbury, 2023). Follow her on X @RachelNuwer.*

Kindness Can Have Unexpectedly Positive Consequences

By Amit Kumar

Scientists who study happiness know that being kind to others can improve well-being. Acts as simple as buying a cup of coffee for someone can boost a person's mood, for example. Everyday life affords many opportunities for such actions, yet people do not always take advantage of them.

In studies published online in the *Journal of Experimental Psychology: General*, Nicholas Epley, a behavioral scientist at the University of Chicago Booth School of Business, and I examined a possible explanation: people who perform random acts of kindness underestimate how much recipients value their behavior.

Across multiple experiments involving approximately 1,000 participants, people performed a random act of kindness—that is, an action done with the primary intention of making someone else (who isn't expecting the gesture) feel good. Those who perform such actions expect nothing in return.

From one situation to the next, the specific acts of kindness varied. For instance, in one experiment, people wrote notes to friends and family "just because." In another, they gave cupcakes away. Across these experiments, we asked both the person performing a kind act and the one receiving it to fill out questionnaires.

We asked the person who had acted with kindness to report their own experience and to predict their recipient's response. Because we wanted to understand how valuable people perceived these acts to be, we asked both the performer and the recipient to rate how "big" the act seemed. In some cases, we also inquired about the actual or perceived cost in time, money or effort. In all cases, we compared a given performer's expectations of the recipient's mood with the recipient's *actual* experience.

Across our investigations, several robust patterns emerged. For one, both performers and recipients of the acts of kindness were in more positive moods than normal after these exchanges. For another, it was clear that performers undervalued their impact: recipients felt significantly better than the kind actors expected. The recipients also reliably rated these acts as "bigger" than the people performing them did.

We initially studied acts of kindness done for familiar people, such as friends, classmates or family. But we found that participants underestimated their positive impact on strangers as well. In one experiment, participants at an ice-skating rink in a public park gave away hot chocolate on a cold winter's day. Again, the experience was more positive than the givers anticipated for the recipients, who were people who just happened to be nearby. Although the people giving out the hot chocolate saw the act as relatively inconsequential, it really mattered to the recipients.

Our research also revealed one reason that people may underestimate their action's impact. When we asked one set of participants to estimate how much someone would like getting a cupcake simply for participating in a study, for example, their predictions were well calibrated with recipients' reactions. But when people received cupcakes through a random act of kindness, the cupcake givers underestimated how positive their recipients would feel. Recipients of these unexpected actions tend to focus more on *warmth* than performers do.

Missing the importance of warmth may stand in the way of being kinder in daily life. People know that cupcakes can make folks feel good, to be sure, but it turns out that cupcakes given in kindness can make them feel *surprisingly* good. If people undervalue this effect, they might not bother to carry out these warm, prosocial behaviors.

And kindness can be contagious. In another experiment, we had people play an economic game that allowed us to examine what are sometimes called "pay it forward" effects. In this game, participants allocated money between themselves and a person whom they would never meet. People who had just been on the receiving end of a kind act gave substantially more to an anonymous person than those who had not. The person who performed the initial act did not recognize that their generosity would spill over in these downstream interactions.

These findings suggest that what might seem small when we are deciding whether to do something nice for someone else could matter a great deal to the person we do it for. Given that these warm gestures can enhance our own mood and brighten the day of another person, why not choose kindness when we can?

This is an opinion and analysis article, and the views expressed by the author or authors are not necessarily those of Scientific American.

About the Author

Amit Kumar is an assistant professor of marketing and psychology at the University of Texas at Austin. He received his A.B. in psychology and economics from Harvard University and his Ph.D. in social psychology from Cornell University.

There Are No Such Things as Gendered Emotions

By Pragya Agarwal

A couple of years ago I was at the ophthalmologist with my six-year-old daughter. The optician asked me more than once, "Why has she been frowning all the time? Why is she so serious?"

I cannot know how much my child's being a girl shaped the optician's thoughts about her emotional state. But I know from my research on the gendering of emotions that people start expecting women and girls to show nurturing and positive expressions early. A different group of researchers analyzed more than 16,000 yearbook photographs of students from kindergarten to college, as well as school faculty and staff. The children showed no significant difference in smiling until age eight or nine, but then the gap started to widen, with girls smiling much more than boys. The difference between girls and boys peaked by the time the students were 14 years old, with girls smiling more frequently and more broadly than boys, and this contrast remained consistent over adulthood.

We may see such results because as children grow older, they become more aware of societal expectations related to gender roles. These expectations could come from peer groups or be imposed on them by parents, teachers or, in the case of the yearbook photos, photographers, both implicitly and explicitly. People may also internalize gender roles portrayed in film and media, where smiling is perceived as more feminine (smiling women are considered more pleasant and friendly) and seriousness is seen as a characteristic of masculinity.

In a different study in which teachers reported their students' emotional expressions, girls were described as having more "peaceful," "calm" and "neutral" expressions (all positive but passive emotions involving little agency), whereas boys showed more "surprise," "curiosity," "anger" and "frustration" (more agentic, or proactive, emotions). It is a widely held misconception that girls are better than boys at regulating their emotions: no neuroscience studies have shown that self-regulatory mechanisms are more developed or active in girls than they are in boys.

Society expects brown women to be more acquiescent and perceives Black women who aren't acquiescent as angry. As a mixed-race girl, my child is likely to encounter some of these stereotypes. A study of American storybooks showed that Hispanic and Latino characters display happiness proportionally more than other characters, whereas white American characters have the space to show displeasure, aligning with the individualistic values of many Western cultures. Children may receive specific messages about emotions while reading storybooks—not only gendered but also culture-specific.

These emotional stereotypes present a double bind for parents hoping to help their children develop emotional intelligence and autonomy. Very early on, children learn to modulate their emotions in line with societal norms they pick up from their peers and caregivers. Regularly suppressing our emotions can massively affect our mental and physical health. Emotional expectations and the offhand comments that children internalize over time harm all kids, irrespective of gender. These expectations can have long-standing negative effects on their sense of self, too. If, however, children do not conform to the behaviors and norms of their membership groups, they may face bullying.

Teaching our children to regulate their emotions is not wrong. Emotional socialization is an important part of parenting to build children's emotional competence and to align them with the values of a particular community. But it is wrong to expect different things from our children based on their gender and race and to minimize or invalidate their emotions based on what we perceive as the correct emotional response. We talk with our children about bodily autonomy; we should also talk about emotional autonomy and how they can better understand and have agency over their own feelings.

Recently I have been reflecting on my relationship with emotions and how I might have endorsed certain expectations through words and actions. According to psychologist John M. Gottman's meta-emotion framework, parents' attitude toward emotions and the way they accept or reject certain ones in themselves affect which emotions they validate in their children.

Many people grew up with very specific emotional rules and model them in their own parenting, consciously or unconsciously. Parents are more likely to validate their child's emotions if they consider those emotions acceptable in general, and they are unlikely to if they believe the cost of expressing the emotion is too high. This cost could be the burden of societal judgment, penalization or ostracization, or it may be an emotional cost the parent pays by having to regulate their own emotions in response.

One study found that mothers were more likely to use emotional language when speaking with four-year-old daughters than with sons that age. Before the start of this experiment, the researchers had observed no difference in emotional understanding and expression between girls and boys, but this changed over the course of the study.

Through the gendered use of language around emotion, children receive a message that certain emotions are more acceptable for girls than for boys and that women talk more about their feelings. Research also shows that parents might react often unconsciously—in a way that encourages emotional expression in girls but discourages emotional expression in boys. These cues might include ignoring, dismissing or invalidating certain emotions in children: anger in girls and sadness in boys.

So many problems emerge from adults' failure to accept the discomfort that comes with children's emotional expression and the way that leads them to set rules for "good girls" and "good boys."

Anyone might be fearful of people judging them in public and seeing them as bad parents who cannot control or discipline their children. We label emotions as "good" or "bad": happiness is good, anger and sadness are bad. And we may discourage or shy away from any "bad" emotions our children express that might make us feel like we are not being good parents. Even our implicit gestures, facial reactions and tone of voice can give children signals from a young age as to which emotions are acceptable and which we should hide away or suppress.

Marc Brackett, director of the Yale Center for Emotional Intelligence, proposes that parents have to find their "best selves" before they can help their children with extreme emotions. From my standpoint, a better approach would be to stop labeling some emotions as "extreme," avoid setting such fixed bounds around emotional expression and not expect children to all conform to the same template.

If we reflected on the messages we internalized while growing up, we could allow ourselves and our children to sit with the discomfort of such "negative" emotions. Over the years, I have realized that it is not my responsibility as a parent to always protect my children from sadness or anger. Children ought to know that such emotions are part of our everyday life–that it is okay to feel sad, frustrated and angry. It is what we do with these emotions that matters.

Teaching children to understand how they are feeling and learn strategies to tackle their emotions is a way of encouraging their emotional autonomy. It is also important for children to know the correct vocabulary so they can name their emotions for themselves and others.

After our visit to the ophthalmologist, my child wondered, "Mummy, should I have been smiling?" I reminded her that she did not have to fake a smile. But even as I have taught her that she doesn't have to modulate or suppress her emotions for anyone else, I have wondered anxiously how much others will judge her for not conforming and what the cost of that will be. I am not suggesting that we each take individual responsibility for resolving the emotional biases in society that perpetuate and enable gender and racial inequities. But we can all reflect on our internal emotional framework and challenge emotional norms, acknowledging that we might be enforcing some of these arbitrary rules, without even realizing it, through our words and our actions.

This is an opinion and analysis article, and the views expressed by the author or authors are not necessarily those of Scientific American.

About the Author

Pragya AgarwalL is a behavioral and data scientist, author of four nonfiction books, a visiting professor of social inequities and injustice at Loughborough University, a fellow at Newnham College, Cambridge University, and a visiting fellow of Black and South Asian history at the University of Oxford. Her latest book is Hysterical: Exploding the Myth of Gendered Emotions *(Canongate, 2022). More at drpragyaagarwal.com and on X: @drpragyaagarwal*

Section 2: Emotions: Helpful or Not?

Negative Emotions Are Key to Well-Being

By Tori Rodriguez

A client sits before me, seeking help untangling his relationship problems. As a psychotherapist, I strive to be warm, nonjudgmental and encouraging. I am a bit unsettled, then, when in the midst of describing his painful experiences, he says, "I'm sorry for being so negative."

A crucial goal of therapy is to learn to acknowledge and express a full range of emotions, and here was a client apologizing for doing just that. In my psychotherapy practice, many of my clients struggle with highly distressing emotions, such as extreme anger, or with suicidal thoughts. In recent years I have noticed an increase in the number of people who also feel guilty or ashamed about what they perceive to be negativity. Such reactions undoubtedly stem from our culture's overriding bias toward positive thinking. Although positive emotions are worth cultivating, problems arise when people start believing they must be upbeat all the time.

In fact, anger and sadness are an important part of life, and new research shows that experiencing and accepting such emotions are vital to our mental health. Attempting to suppress thoughts can backfire and even diminish our sense of contentment. "Acknowledging the complexity of life may be an especially fruitful path to psychological well-being," says psychologist Jonathan M. Adler of the Franklin W. Olin College of Engineering.

Meaningful Misery

Positive thoughts and emotions can, of course, benefit mental health. Hedonic theories define well-being as the presence of positive emotion, the relative absence of negative emotion and a sense of life satisfaction. Taken to an extreme, however, that definition is not congruent with the messiness of real life. In addition, people's outlook can become so rosy that they ignore dangers or become complacent [see "Can Positive Thinking Be Negative?" by Scott O. Lilienfeld and Hal Arkowitz; *Scientific American Mind*, May/June 2011].

Eudaemonic approaches, on the other hand, emphasize a sense of meaning, personal growth and understanding of the self–goals that require confronting life's adversities. Unpleasant feelings are just as crucial as the enjoyable ones in helping you make sense of life's ups and downs. "Remember, one of the primary reasons we have emotions in the first place is to help us evaluate our experiences," Adler says.

Adler and Hal E. Hershfield, a professor of marketing at New York University, investigated the link between mixed emotional experience and psychological welfare in a group of people undergoing 12 sessions of psychotherapy. Before each session, participants completed a questionnaire that assessed their psychological well-being. They also wrote narratives describing their life events and their time in therapy, which were coded for emotional content. As Adler and Hershfield reported in 2012, feeling cheerful and dejected at the same time–for example, "I feel sad at times because of everything I've been through, but I'm also happy and hopeful because I'm working through my issues"–preceded improvements in well-being over the next week or two for subjects, even if the mixed feelings were unpleasant at the time. "Taking the good and the bad together may detoxify the bad experiences, allowing you to make meaning out of them in a way that supports psychological well-being," the researchers found.

Negative emotions also most likely aid in our survival. Bad feelings can be vital clues that a health issue, relationship or other important matter needs attention, Adler points out. The survival value of negative thoughts and emotions may help explain why suppressing them is so fruitless. In a 2009 study psychologist David J. Kavanagh of Queensland University of Technology in Australia and his colleagues asked people in treatment for alcohol abuse and addiction to complete a questionnaire that assessed their drinking-related urges and cravings, as well as any attempts to suppress thoughts related to booze over the previous 24 hours. They found that those who often fought against intrusive alcohol-related thoughts actually harbored more of them. Similar findings from a 2010 study suggested that pushing back negative emotions could spawn more emotional overeating than simply recognizing that you were, say, upset, agitated or blue.

Even if you successfully avoid contemplating a topic, your subconscious may still dwell on it. In a 2011 study psychologist Richard A. Bryant and his colleagues at the University of New South Wales in Sydney told some participants, but not others, to suppress an unwanted thought prior to sleep. Those who tried to muffle the thought reported dreaming about it more, a phenomenon called dream rebound.

Suppressing thoughts and feelings can even be harmful. In a 2012 study psychotherapist Eric L. Garland of Florida State University and his associates measured a stress response based on heart rate in 58 adults in treatment for alcohol dependence while exposing them to alcohol-related cues. Subjects also completed a measure of their tendency to suppress thoughts. The researchers found that those who restrained their thinking more often had stronger stress responses to the cues than did those who suppressed their thoughts less frequently.

Accepting the Pain

Instead of backing away from negative emotions, accept them. Acknowledge how you are feeling without rushing to change your emotional state. Many people find it helpful to breathe slowly and deeply while learning to tolerate strong feelings or to imagine the feelings as floating clouds, as a reminder that they will pass. I often tell my clients that a thought is just a thought and a feeling just a feeling, nothing more.

If the emotion is overwhelming, you may want to express how you feel in a journal or to another person. The exercise may shift your perspective and bring a sense of closure. If the discomfort lingers, consider taking action. You may want to tell a friend her comment was hurtful or take steps to leave the job that makes you miserable.

You may also try doing mindfulness exercises to help you become aware of your present experience without passing judgment on it. One way to train yourself to adopt this state is to focus on your breathing while meditating and simply acknowledge any fleeting thoughts or feelings. This practice may make it easier to accept unpleasant thoughts [see "Being in the Now," by Amishi P. Jha; *Scientific American Mind*, March/April 2013]. Earlier this year Garland and his colleagues found that among 125 individuals with a history of trauma who were also in treatment for substance dependence, those who were naturally more mindful both coped better with their trauma and craved their drug less. Likewise, in a 2012 study psychologist Shannon Sauer-Zavala of Boston University and her co-workers found that a therapy that included mindfulness training helped individuals overcome anxiety disorders. It worked not by minimizing the number of negative feelings but by training patients to accept those feelings.

"It is impossible to avoid negative emotions altogether because to live is to experience setbacks and conflicts," Sauer-Zavala says. Learning how to cope with those emotions is the key, she adds. Indeed, once my client accepted his thoughts and feelings, shaking off his shame and guilt, he saw his problems with greater clarity and proceeded down the path to recovery.

About the Author

Tori Rodriguez is a journalist and psychotherapist based in Atlanta. Her writing has also appeared in the Atlantic, Women's Health *and* Real Simple.

A Newly Discovered Brain Signal Marks Recovery from Depression

By Ingrid Wickelgren

On February 4, 2019, before he was wheeled into the operating room, Tyler Hajjar, then age 28, hugged his mother and quipped, "It's just brain surgery." Hajjar, a resident of Johns Creek, Ga., had traveled to Emory University in Atlanta to outfit his brain with a device that might reset it in hopes of easing the depression that had severely diminished his quality of life—and, at times, threatened that life—for a decade. "Sometimes the best thing I could do was literally just lay in bed all day," he recalls of his long illness, "but honestly, that was better than anything else that was going through my mind—which would have been irreversible."

Hajjar wasn't afraid of the surgery itself—only that it wouldn't work. More than 20 medications, by his count, hadn't helped him in any durable way; neither had electroconvulsive therapy, transcranial magnetic stimulation (TMS) or ketamine infusions.

But there was reason for optimism. Since the first trials in the early 2000s, deep-brain stimulation (DBS), in the hands of expert teams such as the one at Emory, has led to lasting relief in dozens of people with treatment-resistant depression. The technique, which remains experimental for depression—it did not meet the threshold for success in two large randomized controlled clinical trials—involves effectively rebooting the brain using implanted electrodes that stimulate it with pulses of electricity.

Though Hajjar hoped for a clinical benefit, his surgery was designed to also help uncover something novel: a wellness signal from the brain. He and nine others received a device that not only delivered electricity to the brain but also sensed neural activity. Analyzing that activity and correlating it with clinical ratings yielded a biomarker that signaled when a person was better in an enduring way.

The results, reported on September 20 in *Nature*, reveal a neural code that represents the first known signal of the presence or absence of depression in the brain. "This is to me, studying depression for more than 30 years, the closest clue to know, fundamentally, 'What is depression, and how do we think about how the brain can be repaired?'" says Helen Mayberg, a neurologist at the Icahn School of Medicine at Mount Sinai, who was co-senior author of the study.

The new biomarker could improve the efficacy of the technology because it tells doctors when a person's symptoms call for an adjustment in the stimulation and when they don't–and, if tested further, it might even serve as a predictor of depression relapse. With such guidance, a larger number of doctors could capably care for people who have undergone DBS. "It could be very useful to bedside clinicians and to making the therapy more scalable, more effective and, frankly, helping the physician to do no harm," says Michael Okun, a neurologist at the University of Florida, who was not involved in the study. Okun is a co-founder of the DBS Think Tank, an annual forum centered on cutting-edge issues involving the technology. Nearly three million people in the U.S. have treatment-resistant depression and stand to benefit from an approved therapy.

The work also could spur advances in less invasive treatments that modulate brain activity, such as TMS (which involves placing a coil on the scalp to create a magnetic field), says Gordon Baltuch, a neurosurgeon at Columbia University Irving Medical Center, who did not participate in the new research. "Neuromodulation could potentially help a cohort of people who have a disease which is not only disabling but is fatal" to tens of thousands of people each year in the U.S., Baltuch says.

Other biomarkers for depression could follow if, say, changes in a person's face or voice, or in brain waves detected at the surface of the brain, correlate with the internal signal. Study investigators found a pattern of facial expressions that changed in tandem with the brain's state, which is a promising sign. "There are probably many ways we will be able to read out from the brain, invasively and noninvasively," says Christopher Rozell, a neuroengineer at

Georgia Institute of Technology, who identified the wellness signal and was co-senior author on the new study. "It opens the floodgates for people to be able to look for these sorts of signals."

The subcallosal cingulate, also known as "Brodmann area 25," is embedded deep in the brain, above and behind the eyes. It is a critical crossroads for four major nerve fiber tracts and thus an intersection of brain traffic coming from areas that control all the functions that go awry in depression—emotional regulation, sleep, appetite, reward, motivation and memory, among others.

Two decades ago Mayberg was mapping brain circuits involved in depression and noticed that every time an antidepressant worked, area 25 became less active. So she decided to see if stimulating the brain there could modulate the area's activity and ease depression in the most intractable cases, where other treatments had failed. Over the course of 20 years, she and her teams found that it could. In a 2019 follow-up study on 28 people treated with DBS, for example, Mayberg and her colleagues reported that half or more of the individuals significantly improved, and about 30 percent achieved remission and stayed well two to eight years later. One patient of Mayberg's has stayed in remission for 18 years. "People just don't get better; they stay better," Mayberg says. Response rates have now climbed to about 80 percent as new techniques enable better targeting of area 25 in individual brains, Mayberg says.

Although Mayberg knew the treatment worked, at least in her patients, she did not know how. In 2013 Mayberg, then at Emory, heard about prototype stimulators made by the medical device company Medtronic that could also record from the brain, and she applied to receive 10 of them. She teamed up with Rozell and his colleagues, who had the skills to make sense of what the sensors were picking up.

In 2015 Emory neurosurgeons implanted the first of the new devices by threading one electrode into area 25 in each hemisphere and connecting these to a pacemaker. Each electrode has four contacts, places where it interfaces with brain tissue around area 25. Four years later Hajjar was the last member of this cohort to have the operation. In the operating room, he was awakened briefly, and he reported that stimulation of one of the contacts on the left side of the brain brought on a new feeling of emotional lightness–one that would, if he weren't bolted in, enable him to go out with his father to a shooting range to participate in an activity that they both enjoyed.

It was a promising sign. Over the course of six months, the device collected data from Hajjar's brain and picked up a constellation of brain waves that reflected the combined activity of thousands of neurons. "Like a symphony where you have some high-pitched instruments and some low-pitched instruments, we can take these brain signals and decompose them into frequencies in different ranges," Rozell says.

Hajjar and the others in the study also had a weekly clinical assessment, which was videotaped. Within a couple of months, most participants felt somewhat better. After six months, symptoms had diminished by at least half in nine of the 10 individuals, and seven achieved remission. Only six of them, however, had usable brain data, and five of the six showed the typical pattern of improvement.

Using data from those five people, Rozell and his team built artificial intelligence software to compare participants' brain wave patterns at the start of the study, when they were sick, with those patterns at the end, when they were better. The researchers found a coordinated change in a few frequency bands that could distinguish a sick brain from a brain that was well with 90 percent accuracy. "It's the very first time that we've really been able to get a brain readout of recovery," Rozell says.

The signal was the same for all the participants, but it showed up at different times: at eight weeks in one person and at 20 weeks in another, for example. When a doctor sees it, they know that regardless of their patient's current state of mind, they can leave the stimulation as is, says Patricio Riva-Posse, the study's lead psychiatrist. "There is an objective biomarker beyond my impression as a psychiatrist that can tell me, 'Oh yes, this patient is slowly getting better,'" Riva-Posse says. It can also provide people being treated reassurance that they are on the right path. "We have a goal line for recovery," Mayberg says.

The sixth participant with usable brain data showed an atypical trajectory after treatment. She felt better after the operation and stayed well for four months, but then she relapsed. The scientists looked for the wellness signal in her after the fact. She had it at the start of her treatment, but it disappeared a month before she relapsed–and so it could have served as a warning sign. "If we would have had it, we would have turned up [her stimulation] a month earlier. She might not have gotten into trouble," Mayberg says.

Using artificial intelligence software, the researchers also found changes in a person's face that paralleled the appearance of the brain's wellness signal. Those changes fell short of a clinically useful biomarker, Rozell says, because the study was too small to define a pattern that was both specific for depression and common to all participants. Still, the finding points to the possibility of a more universal indicator of recovery. "We will build models that aren't just for my small cohort of lucky patients but that could generalize to everybody," Mayberg says.

Brain scans might also offer clues to wellness. Scans of the study participants' brain before their surgery showed that the degree of damage to certain nerve fiber tracts correlated with the severity of their depression. The researchers could not look for a change in those tracts with the treatment, however, because the participants could not be put in a brain scanner once the implant was in place.

The latest DBS technology is compatible with brain imaging. A team at Mount Sinai has now implanted some of these new devices in another group of 10 participants and will look not only for the wellness biomarker but also for evidence of a repaired brain circuit, Mayberg says.

Formal approval of DBS for depression requires randomized controlled clinical trials. One earlier such trial targeting area 25 did not demonstrate a benefit over a sham procedure when its sponsor, St. Jude Medical (now Abbott), halted it in 2013 at the halfway point. Yet some people improved after the stopping point, and the accumulated results and lessons from small trials leave a lot of room for hope, experts say. (Another trial targeting a different place in the brain using a DBS system from Medtronic also had disappointing results.)

Despite these setbacks, the technology has not been abandoned as a depression treatment. "It's a multibillion-dollar industry. People are going to keep trying until they get it," Okun says. "They are getting closer, and the data is getting better and better as they see these groups improving their outcomes."

Abbott is gearing up for a do-over. In July 2022 the U.S. Food and Drug Administration granted the company a breakthrough device designation for the use of the company's DBS system in treatment-resistant depression, thereby expediting its development and, if all goes well, eventual approval. Abbott is now working with the FDA on a plan for a clinical trial, according to Jenn Wong, the company's divisional vice president of global clinical and regulatory affairs in their neuromodulation business.

At the six-month mark, Hajjar went into remission. He started hanging out with friends he hadn't seen in a while and was able to take on some temporary work. "I felt like I could get back into the world," he recalls. He still struggled with anxiety, however, and in 2021 his depression began to reemerge. But adjustments to the stimulation brought him back.

Hajjar is now employed part-time and has had several speaking gigs in which he has shared his story with surgeons, scientists and medical students at conferences or over Zoom. He is even making tentative plans for the future–including pursuing his long-term interest in mechanical drafting. Perhaps most importantly, he has a new outlook on life. "I look forward to waking up in the morning," he says.

About the Author

Ingrid Wickelgren is a freelance science journalist based in New Jersey.

Suppressing an Onrush of Toxic Thoughts Might Improve Your Mental Health

By Ingrid Wickelgren

Zulkayda Mamat is no stranger to traumatic memories. Ethnically Uighur, Mamat left China at age 12 after an uprising in the region of East Turkestan, where most of Mamat's extended family still lives. More than one million Uighurs have been arbitrarily detained in "political education" camps and prisons. "I know people in camps. I have witnessed families completely broken down, people in the diaspora, their entire lives changed," says Mamat, who just received her doctorate in cognitive neuroscience from the University of Cambridge.

Over the years, Mamat has noticed how the most resilient Uighurs she knows manage to cope with their trauma. Their formula is simple: they push the distressing memories out of their mind. Mamat herself is good at this. "It's almost intuitive to be able to control my thoughts," she says.

Clinical psychologists often warn against suppressing thoughts because they believe distressing ideas and images will bubble up later with greater frequency and worsen mental health problems. Psychoanalysis focuses on the contrasting approach of hunting down and exploring the meaning of any thoughts a person might have pushed to the back of their mind.

But Mamat now has data to support her intuition that suppression is beneficial. In a September 20 paper in *Science Advances*, she and her adviser, cognitive neuroscientist Michael Anderson, report that they successfully trained people—many of whom had mental health problems—to suppress their fears and that doing so improved these individuals' mental health. "Suppressing negative thoughts, far from being a hazardous thing to do," Anderson says, "actually seemed to be of great benefit, especially to the people who need it the most—people suffering from depression, anxiety and post-traumatic stress."

The work also calls into question whether people with mental health disorders have an inherent inability to suppress intrusive thoughts. "It's probably not a deficit," Mamat says. The vast majority of people in the study, she says, "were surprised to see that this was something they could learn."

The technique bears a likeness to behavioral therapies in which people expose themselves to cues or situations that trigger fear and anxiety—heights, dirt or parties, say—until the brain learns to inhibit those fear responses, says Charan Ranganath, a cognitive neuroscientist at the University of California, Davis, who was not involved in the research. But learning to halt the thoughts that arise from those cues is a novel approach. "What's surprising to me is telling people to stop that thought in and of itself is effective," Ranganath says. "That's an idea that could be really useful to bring into therapies."

Not everyone agrees that the approach is safe or likely to be successful as a therapeutic tool. But if further research suggests it is, suppression training might either be used alone or in conjunction with, say, cognitive-behavioral or exposure therapy, Anderson suggests.

The new findings stand in stark contrast to the conventional wisdom that thought suppression is both ineffective and harmful as a therapeutic approach. In the 1980s psychologist Daniel Wegner popularized this idea with his "white bear" experiments. In these studies, people were instructed not to think about a white bear. And in following those instructions, they later thought about white bears more often than did participants in a control group who had been initially told to think about the animals. Trying not to think about something, Wegner concluded, causes those same thoughts to pop up more often.

The idea has been influential in clinical psychology. Anderson and his colleagues, however, have generated data spanning two decades that suggest that pushing away negative memories causes those memories to fade and become less distressing. His experiments are meant to mimic a real-world scenario in which people encounter reminders of worrying thoughts and then need to decide whether to stem those thoughts or dwell on them.

Previously Anderson had not directly tested whether his technique, which he calls retrieval suppression, could be useful as a therapy. One potential problem was that the people with mental health conditions, who could benefit most from such a therapy, might be incapable of practicing it because of the way their brain functioned. Some data supported that idea, but Mamat was not convinced it was true. She thought anyone might be able to learn to stem their thoughts if they were shown how.

In March 2020 she decided to find out. COVID had halted all in-person research, including the brain-imaging project Mamat had been pursuing. It had also spawned a wave of anxiety, depression and other mental health problems that needed to be addressed. Mamat told Anderson she wanted to test a therapy involving suppression that she could administer online from her apartment.

She cast a wide net for participants. English-speaking adults could volunteer as long as they were not color blind and did not have a neurological disorder or reading disability–and many of the volunteers did have mental health problems. Of the 120 people from 16 countries who participated in the study, 43 percent had clinically concerning levels of anxiety, 18 percent had significant depressive symptoms and 24 percent had probable post-traumatic stress disorder (PTSD).

Before the training, Mamat asked each person to generate thoughts on which to base a set of cue words: 20 specific worries and fears that repeatedly intruded on their thoughts, 36 neutral events and 20 wishes for the future. As part of the study, the researchers took assessments of the participants' anxiety, depression, worry and well-being.

Over three days, 61 of the participants were exposed to the cue words that represented their fears. For example, if someone was afraid that their parents would be hospitalized with COVID, the cue word might be "hospital." During training, they were instructed to stare at the reminder for several seconds and acknowledge the event but then to shut down all thoughts about it, as well as any associated imagery. If thoughts, feelings or images did spring to mind, participants were to immediately push those ideas out of awareness and return their attention to the reminder. They were not to generate distracting thoughts because the researchers did not want any type of avoidance to be part of the strategy. A control group of 59 people were instructed to do the same for neutral events such as being seen by an optician.

In other trials, participants were told to conjure imagery to embellish and elaborate either neutral or positive events. The two groups suppressed each fear or neutral event or imagined each hope or neutral event 12 times each day for three days and were then tested on both the vividness and emotional impact of their thoughts.

As expected, suppression diminished the vividness and intensity of the fears. As a group, participants recalled details of their personal fears or neutral events less often and experienced reduced anxiety related to those fears.

More notably, suppressing fears improved people's mental health and did so much more than suppressing neutral scenarios. Worry, depression and anxiety were all significantly reduced, and well-being increased. "What the training seems to be doing is giving people a way to stop from going into this vortex of worry when a negative thought comes up," Ranganath says. Surprisingly, imagining positive events produced no mental health benefits, suggesting that generating positive thoughts has far less power than blocking negative thoughts, Anderson says.

The researchers also showed that suppression did not lead memories to rebound, as the white bear experiments might suggest. Although there were individuals whose anxiety or depression worsened after training, there were fewer such cases in the group suppressing thoughts of feared events than among individuals who were blocking out neutral events. The researchers "went above and beyond" to demonstrate that the therapy did not have adverse effects, Ranganath says.

Three months after the training, depression scores continued to decline for the group as a whole. On measures of anxiety, worry and PTSD, however, the effects of the training were only apparent among the people who had been depressed or anxious or showed signs of PTSD at the start of the study. "The people who were suffering at the outset showed a consistent benefit," Anderson says.

It appears that the more symptomatic a person had been, the more likely they were to use suppression after training, apparently because they found it useful. (No one was told to practice the technique after the three-day training period.) Among those with probable PTSD, for example, 82 percent reported reduced anxiety, and 63 percent said their mood improved–changes they attributed to suppression. "It's the people who were suffering at the outset who saw how much suppression benefited them," Anderson says.

Participants also reported that the training improved their ability to suppress thoughts; they rated their skill on the third day as much higher than they did on the first. Three quarters of the participants described being surprised or very surprised by their newfound faculty. "I couldn't believe how effective it was, and it made me realize how powerful my brain can be," one participant wrote.

The strategy has also drawn criticism, however. "[The paper] may lead some people to conclude that they should practice suppressing memories of a recent traumatic event, which, research suggests, may actually increase their risk of developing posttraumatic stress disorder," says Amanda Draheim, a psychologist at Goucher College in Baltimore.

Fully vetting the technique requires a randomized controlled clinical trial with several hundred participants, something Anderson has in his sights. Mamat has developed a phone app that could be used in such a trial, and she hopes it will eventually be available for widespread use.

During her study, Mamat got to know the participants, talking to them for hours from her apartment over Zoom. One of them broke down in tears and told Mamat that the experience had changed her life. Another described suppression as a "power" and planned to teach it to her children. The personal feedback convinced Mamat that the experiment was worthwhile, no matter what the data showed. "That was enough for me to have done this entire thing," she says. "That was beautiful. That was really beautiful."

About the Author

Ingrid Wickelgren is a freelance science journalist based in New Jersey.

Outrage Fatigue Is Real. These Tips May Help

By Tanya Lewis

You're probably feeling it: the onslaught of depressing news and commentary about political actions, wars, climate disasters and more. The first few times you're exposed to a perceived injustice, you feel fired up and ready to fight against it. But after being repeatedly faced with this moral assault, you start to feel fatigued, even withdrawn. Resistance feels futile.

This phenomenon is informally referred to as "outrage fatigue." While it hasn't been well studied, researchers have studied outrage itself–what purpose it serves and how it spreads. William Brady, an assistant professor of management and organizations at Northwestern University's Kellogg School of Management, and his colleagues recently published a study on how outrage helps misinformation spread online. They found that posts from misinformation sources were more likely than those from trustworthy news outlets to elicit moral outrage (anger and disgust)–and that people were more likely to reshare them without reading them. But extensive exposure to outrage-inducing content can cause feelings of fatigue that turn people off participating in political action, Brady says.

Fortunately, there are ways to combat such fatigue, such as getting involved in local politics or causes. *Scientific American* talked to Brady about why we experience outrage fatigue and what to do about it.

[An edited transcript of the interview follows.]

Q: What is outrage fatigue?

A: When people are experiencing outrage, what that means, theoretically, is they're feeling that there's a transgression that has occurred against their perceived sense of right and wrong–what we might also call a moral norm. Outrage, in a way, is very functional and good for groups, because it helps bring attention to these things that our social group or our culture would consider to be a transgression. And that usually is a good thing, because it helps groups to figure out, "Okay, here's a bad thing happening, and we need to coordinate. We need to catalyze collective action so that we can solve this issue." The reason why outrage tends to work as a tool for that is because it's very arousing–it draws our attention, it gets us worked up, and that can sometimes motivate us to action.

But of course there's a flip side to outrage, which is that when it occurs along the lines of group identities–for example, when you get outraged at a political out-group doing something that is counter-normative or against the moral views of your political group–that can also create hostility, and it can create conflict. Obviously, we've seen that with rising polarization in the U.S., but also in other countries in Europe and around the world. Theoretically, there's this kind of give and take with outrage. It can be helpful; it can be functional. But if you're constantly in that state, it can lead to conflict and escalation of political disputes. Psychologically, if you're constantly in that state it can be very exhausting.

Q: How does outrage play out differently at the group level and the individual level?

A: If at a group level you're constantly outraged and playing out all these transgressions, you can get this kind of group-level fatigue. Moral outrage loses some of its potency because it's hard to know, "What should I focus my outrage on?" It's a limited resource. It requires a lot of attention and resources, so you start to get a little jaded, because you're like, "Well, I'm supposed to be outraged at this and this and this. So what? I don't know what to do."

This has not been empirically studied very well, as far as I know. But we've looked a little bit at people leaving conversations in the context of online conversation. Basically, what happens is, some people are the super–outrage producers, and then other people—which turns out, according to some of my data, to be the majority of responses—don't talk as much because they might feel isolated. Maybe things are getting too intense. Other people just might not know what they should be focusing on. And then there's other people, even—we've seen this on social media, especially—who feel kind of afraid to express an opinion, because if there's a lot of outrage in the environment, you feel like you're going to be targeted if you say slightly the wrong thing.

If you want to talk about it individually, I'm not aware of empirical research that has studied that specifically in response to recent political events. This is now getting into the realm of speculation, but there is some research that shows that when people are feeling a lot of negative emotions in general—I'd obviously consider outrage in that bucket—they tend to feel like they need to regulate their emotions, because it can be taxing on them.

Q: Would it be fair to say that individuals often behave as part of a bigger group—whether it's political party or race or something else—and we feel a threat to our group whenever something happens that seems negative toward that broader group?

A: Yeah, 100 percent, and this is very well studied in social psychology. I think the key thing to understand is that we flexibly identify ourselves depending on the context. During a political election, when we see our group lose, social identity theory would predict that this would be a case when you very strongly are prone to identifying with categorizing yourself. For example: "Oh, I'm a Democrat. I feel very saliently my Democrat identity, so now I feel threatened. We just lost the election. Trump is saying he's going to do all this stuff that my group wouldn't do." Then you're very likely to feel outrage and other emotions on behalf of your group, and that's where the threat comes in.

But my point in saying that it's flexible is just to say it's interesting to think about how we might then go into another context, and now our categorization is slightly different, or maybe we're just feeling a certain identity that doesn't have to do with politics. And now we're realizing, like, "Man, I've been in this chronically group-identified state with my political identity, and I have been really outraged, and it is taking a toll on me individually."

Q: How does the media environment, and especially social media, affect the way we experience outrage?

A: A lot of times we can get kind of exhausted from viewing all the outrage we see in a context like social media. And the problem with that is that's actually not necessarily representative of how people are feeling in our political group. What my research shows is that when you combine the use of engagement-based algorithms that are on X, Meta, etc., they are disproportionately amplifying outrage content. And what that means in practice is that even if there's this small minority group of highly motivated political users who are posting a lot of this stuff, in fact, most people aren't. The algorithms amplify, and it makes it look as if there are a ton of people doing it. To me, that's concerning, because then we might get turned off of political participation. We feel like we're already kind of exhausted by the general media and the anger and politics. But in fact that's not actually representative of our group.

Q: Is there anything we can do to combat outrage fatigue? How can people healthily disengage to some extent?

A: I think people really have to figure out, "How can I be aware and experience outrage while also grounding myself in local communities?" Because I think local community politics is how you can build a kind of feeling of safety and understanding among a group, like, "Oh, actually, there are concrete things I can do, or we can do, to organize and think about how we challenge the status quo we disagree with." I think the problem is we're in a kind of era where a primary way that, especially, young people engage in politics is through these online, honestly not that personal, spaces. And I think it's been problematic for the kind of cross-coalition building that used to occur when there was just more organizing in offline spaces.

So I think it's just getting more involved at a local level, where you have this interpersonal connection. It doesn't cost much to express outrage online. It's much more costly to try and get involved in the community and to have more direct and focused outrage. Directed outrage is less likely to lead to fatigue because there's a satisfaction of knowing what it's going for, and there are concrete outcomes you're looking for.

Q: Can limiting your media consumption help?

A: There are some deactivation studies for social media specifically [studies in which participants deactivate their account for some period of time].To be honest, there are kind of mixed results. One study showed a decrease in polarization, but people lost some political knowledge. Another study showed there was no effect. And there's a big multicountry study going on with that, but to be honest, these studies tend to look at, like, two weeks of deactivation. It's hard to say, "Is it a good or bad thing?" It's something that is nuanced. But what I would say, drawing from what I know from my research, is that people do have the ability to alter their social media ecosystem. If you feel like you're getting too much outrage and bombarded with stuff in a way that is not productive or is causing fatigue then you have the ability to change that environment by engaging with different content.

Q: Is there evidence that political parties or groups weaponize outrage fatigue as a way of making people less engaged or resistant?

A: In general, here's one thing we know from at least the U.S. context: outrage has been used as a political tool to divide groups. For example, the political right has specifically used outrage stoking to get certain groups who would be harmed by their economic policies—say, the working class—to vote for them on other issues that have nothing to do with that. For example, issues of immigration, race, identity, things that make them outraged. Abortion is another one—it can distract people from other issues that would harm them. Two of our studies looked at the Russian disinformation organization the Internet Research Agency that was specifically using that as a strategy in the 2016 and 2020 elections. So we know that outrage as a divisive tool is something that is used as a strategy for sure.

About the Author

Tanya Lewis is a senior editor covering health and medicine at Scientific American. *She writes and edits stories for the website and print magazine on topics ranging from COVID to organ transplants. She also appears on* Scientific American's *podcast* Science, Quickly *and writes* Scientific American's *weekly Health & Biology newsletter. She has held a number of positions over her eight years at* Scientific American, *including health editor, assistant news editor and associate editor at* Scientific American Mind. *Previously, she has written for outlets that include* Insider, Wired, Science News, *and others. She has a degree in biomedical engineering from Brown University and one in science communication from the University of California, Santa Cruz. Follow her on Bluesky: @tanyalewis.bsky.social*

Can Outrage Be a Good Thing?

By Victoria Spring

Lately, it has started to feel as if outrage is everywhere. On both sides of the political aisle, people have taken to social media–and to the streets–to express their fury over perceived injustices. The religious right demands a boycott against a popular coffee chain for removing religious iconography from their holiday cups; meanwhile, the left rallies marches in protest against police brutality against young Black men. In the midst of all this anger, both liberal and conservative pundits have started raising the question: has outrage drowned out civil dialogue in America?

The moment you read the title of this article, you likely had an immediate, gut-level reaction. Perhaps you thought *of course, outrage helps get things done!* Or maybe you thought *that's ridiculous, outrage just drives people further apart*. I would venture to guess, though, that most people have an intuition that outrage is ultimately a bad thing–that it gets in the way of constructive dialogue, further dividing our increasingly-partisan nation.

A similar discussion has been going on in psychology, in two separate subfields: moral psychology (the scientific study of how we judge what's right and wrong) and intergroup psychology (the study of how different groups–e.g., genders, races/ethnicities, religions–interact). As those of you who voted for option number two–"outrage is bad"–might have predicted, some research from moral psychology suggests outrage drives disproportionately aggressive behavior against wrongdoers. But on the flip side, and consistent with "outrage is good" option number one, work in intergroup psychology demonstrates outrage can serve as a glue binding people together in activism against injustice–increased anger predicts support for non-violent solutions to intractable conflicts like the one between Israel and Palestine.

So if the experimental results on outrage are mixed, what's the truth about outrage?

This is the question that inspired me—and my colleagues Daryl Cameron and Mina Cikara—to write a paper (now out in *Trends in Cognitive Sciences*) aimed at untangling the mixed research on outrage. In the paper, we suggest that maybe the problem is how we've been thinking about outrage to begin with. So much of the dialogue about moral outrage seems to be about whether outrage as an *emotion* is fundamentally "good" or "bad." Pundits and politicians accuse those on the other side of the political aisle of "fauxoutrage"—manufactured anger over perceived injustices. Even in psychology, researchers have suggested moral outrage is just a thin façade disguising more egotistical motives (e.g., to "virtue signal"). Even the term we use to describe outrage—calling it *moral* outrage, specifically—might bias us toward viewing outrage itself as a moral act.

Perhaps "is outrage good or bad?" is not the question we should be asking. After all, emotions aren't moral or immoral in and of themselves. The only thing that can be good or bad is what you *do* with that emotion. What if we approached outrage functionally instead, and asked: when can the expression of outrage be viewed as positive or negative? And when is outrage most effectively leveraged toward social change ... or social destruction?

Our tendency to view outrage-the-emotion as a behavior that can be "right" or "wrong" has some pretty bad downsides. If outrage is something that can be moralized, that means we can get mad at people for experiencing it. And instead of being upset about a moral transgression, the condemnation of that transgression starts to be seen as the "real" immorality. Take for example the entrenched tendency for majority group members to respond with defensiveness and anger when they're accused of prejudice. The accuser's outrage starts to be seen as somehow worse than the prejudice that inspired it. Discounting the accuser's anger protects the accused from accountability—after all, "faux" outrage hardly deserves a respectful response—while redirecting blame toward the victim instead of the perpetrator.

And unfortunately, this moralization of outrage tends to be more frequently wielded against marginalized people, making it even more dangerous. To start with, certain groups are actually perceived as angrier *in general* than other groups. Take for example the stereotype of the "angry Black woman." Black women are perceived as expressing inappropriate anger more frequently than people from other groups, potentially contributing to mental health treatment disparities. Black men aren't exempt–according to political scientists, stereotypes about Black men and uncontrollable anger shape the way Black politicians have to present themselves in the public eye, because even mild anger expressed by a Black man will be perceived as extreme.

This doesn't just apply to Black people, though. Research suggests that marginalized people in general are held to higher moral standards than majority group members. Specifically, this work found that marginalized people were expected to be more tolerant of immigrants–and if they weren't, they were judged as more immoral than majority group members who were equally intolerant. In other words: moral outrage about immigration is judged more harshly when it's being expressed by minority group members

Does that mean that marginalized group members should avoid expressing anger, so their anger isn't overdramatized and used as a weapon against them? Perhaps. But some scholars argue that trying to decrease anger for the sake of social harmony only ultimately serves to reinforce an inequitable status quo. Meanwhile, marginalized people's anger can serve as a catalyst joining group members together to fight against injustice and oppression–and suppressing that anger can suppress moral agency and resistance against injustice.

As for our second question–when does outrage translate into activism vs. aggression–that remains to be seen. Although we've established outrage has the potential to produce both destructive and constructive outcomes, researchers still need to do more work to understand what conditions encourage people to express their outrage as collective action (or as collective violence). We do know that anger, specifically, is a key factor in reducing discrimination–research has demonstrated that anger about discrimination specifically drives reductions in bias against minorities. To the degree that reduced discrimination produces more positive intergroup social behavior, this might be more evidence in favor of how anger can produce positive outcomes.

One thing is clear: I can't tell you if outrage is "good" or "bad." Outrage is an emotion, not a behavior itself–emotions can't be moralized. Like all emotions, outrage can be used as a weapon ... or a tool.

About the Author

Victoria Spring is a fifth-year doctoral student in psychology at The Pennsylvania State University. Victoria is interested in social emotions–particularly empathy and anger–and how emotions and group dynamics interact to produce moral judgments.

Anger Can Help You Meet Your Goals

By Heather Lench

You may be having a perfectly ordinary day when suddenly you see an upsetting news story and feel overwhelmed by fury. Or you're trying to have a calm conversation about an important issue and abruptly find yourself crying. These moments can make people feel out of control, and the emotions involved can feel bad or uncomfortable in themselves.

That gives negative emotions a bad reputation: they're often seen as dangerous or destructive. People try to avoid them, suppress them or ignore them. But research reveals that negative emotions are useful for people and important for a successful and satisfying life. Negative emotions are sets of organized responses that occur when something people care about is not going well, and, psychologists have found, those responses can help people *improve* their situation.

In a recent series of studies, my colleagues and I tested this idea for the case of anger. Past work had shown that people feel angry when they confront an obstacle or a challenge to goals–for instance, a computer that crashes repeatedly while a person is trying to complete a project. Sometimes the obstacle is another person, who might challenge progress through resistance or injustice, such as a boss who does not give a deserved pay raise. In these situations, people get mad. A host of changes occur across physiology, cognition and behavior when we're angry: the emotion alters our body, our thinking and the actions we are likely to take.

We wondered: Could anger and its accompanying transformations *help* people do better in situations that involve obstacles or challenges?

We designed a series of experiments with more than 1,000 participants. In most of the scenarios we used, people first completed a task designed to make them angry, such as viewing insulting images or tackling a frustrating computer assignment. In comparison, other participants did tasks that made them feel neutral or some emotion other than anger. For instance, images of household items evoked no specific emotions, whereas images of people crying elicited sadness. Afterward, all participants completed separate tasks that involved a clear goal, along with a challenge to that goal, such as solving a tricky anagram or playing a difficult game.

Repeatedly we found that people who got mad first were more successful than the other participants in the challenges that followed. Angry people persisted longer and did better at solving word problems, for instance. They also scored better on a challenging video game and were more likely to sign a petition to stop student tuition increases. We also considered a real-world case by looking at survey data collected from 989 people during the 2016 and 2020 U.S. general elections. We found that a person's anger at an opposing candidate's potential win predicted greater likelihood that a person would vote in the next election.

Across our studies, anger helped achieve challenging goals. When the goals were not challenging, getting angry did not improve outcomes. For example, when participants had to solve easy word puzzles or play a simple video game that involved making a single jump, participants who were angry fared no better than those in other conditions.

But what does this mean for people's life? Here the story becomes more complicated. The findings do not mean that everyone should get riled up in order to achieve their goals. But anger clearly can be useful in overcoming obstacles.

Part of the challenge with learning from our emotions is that they are not directional–that is, they do not necessarily push us toward a specific type of action to resolve a situation. We designed our experimental studies to have a clear goal with only a singular action or choice involved (such as persist or give up). Life is typically much more complicated, and people have many actions to choose from. Some of those options can have serious negative consequences.

Rage at a crashing computer could motivate someone to take it to a repair shop. But it could also motivate them to smash the computer on the floor. Both actions have removed the obstacle: the crashing computer. Yet only one is truly beneficial in completing the larger project–whatever the person was doing on the computer. This complication in using our negative emotions contributes to their bad reputation. Anger can lead people to do things they would rather not do that don't match their long-term goals.

Indeed, in one of our experiments, we found that angry people were more likely to cheat when given the chance than other study participants. Cheating gave those players an edge, but it's also unethical. As another example, past research has found that expressing anger can make others concede and give in to demands. Although using this intense emotion to fuel an impassioned, persuasive argument could be beneficial, if a person who gets upset ends up bullying others, this will ultimately have negative repercussions for their relationships.

Fortunately, there is a lot of research on how to improve responses to emotions that can guide us with our anger as well. Because this powerful emotion is a signal that we have encountered a challenge to a goal we care about, the best response is to stop, orient to what's happening and consider the best way to respond to achieve the desired outcome.

Ask yourself: What is my goal? Then choose actions that align with it. In an argument with a romantic partner, if your long-term aim is to improve the relationship, anger can motivate appropriate next steps, including expressing your needs, working to a compromise and listening. But if the goal that drives you is to prove your point in the argument, you may speak louder, ignore your partner's perspective and act aggressively. Taking a moment to check on one's immediate and long-term aims can help prevent detrimental responses and prompt better ones.

Negative emotions aren't bad. They are incredibly important indicators that significant events are taking place. So the next time one happens, don't push it away—pay attention.

This is an opinion and analysis article, and the views expressed by the author or authors are not necessarily those of Scientific American.

About the Author

Heather Lench is a professor of psychological and brain sciences at Texas A&M University.

Grief Is a Learning Experience

By Claudia Christine Wolf

Why does it hurt so much to lose someone you love? What happens in your brain as it strives to cope? Pioneering psychologist Mary-Frances O'Connor worked on one of the first neuroimaging studies of grief more than two decades ago. She and her colleagues found that a loved one's absence means a major disruption not only to our life but also within our brain.

O'Connor now runs the Grief, Loss and Social Stress (GLASS) Lab at the University of Arizona, where she tries to tease out the biological mechanisms underlying grief. In particular, she studies prolonged grief, a state in which people don't seem to heal, instead staying immersed in their loss for years. In her book *The Grieving Brain* (HarperOne, 2022), O'Connor explains how insight into brain circuits and neurotransmitters can enable us to navigate bereavement with self-compassion. "Grief is the cost of loving someone," she writes. When a loved one dies, it can feel like we've lost a part of ourselves because their presence is coded into our neurons.

Spektrum der Wissenschaft, Scientific American's German-language sibling publication, spoke with O'Connor about how love permanently changes our neural wiring and what we can do to feel more like ourselves while our brain tries to update its understanding of the world when a loved one is gone.

Q: People who have lost someone often feel like their beloved will walk into the room at any moment, or sometimes they think they're seeing the person on the street. Why does that happen?

A: It's not perfectly worked out yet, but I have what I call the gone-but-also-everlasting theory. We think of the brain as a single entity, but there are many systems in it. On the one hand, you have the memory system, in which, say, we have a memory of being at the bedside or at a funeral. So one stream of information in our brain understands the reality of our loss and can remember that happening. But there's another stream of information in our brain, and that comes from attachment neurobiology.

To understand what happens during loss, we first have to think about what happens during bonding. When that relationship is created, that bond is encoded in the brain in very specific regions and very specific ways. It comes with a belief that "I will always be there for you and you will always be there for me."

That is the nature of a bonded relationship. It is what makes us know our partner will be at home when we return after work or enables us to send our children off to school–we know that they will return to us and that we will seek them out if they, for some reason, don't turn up. The belief that they are out there in the world, even if we can't see them or hear them, works very well when our loved ones are alive.

That attachment neurobiology, that belief in the everlasting nature of the bond, does not change immediately when a loved one dies. That second stream of information is still telling us they're out there. We should go find them because they are missing, because they are lost. And so those two streams of information–the memory of the reality on one hand and, on the other, this belief that they are out there–cannot both be true.

Our brain really struggles to understand what has happened. And when we become aware that we have both beliefs, it causes a lot of distress and grief.

Q: In your book, you also write about the brain as a prediction machine. When it comes to bereavement, is the brain making wrong predictions?

A: Predictions happen at a lot of different levels, because usually our relationships with our loved ones are multifaceted. So the brain is predicting, as I just said, that our loved one is out there, and it is sort of motivating us to go seek them out. It has difficulty learning to predict their absence. If you've woken up next to someone for thousands of days, and you wake up one morning, and they're not there next to you in bed, it's actually not a very good prediction that they have died, right? Our brain would much rather believe, "Oh, they're on a trip, or they've gotten up early today, and they're just not here right now."

In fact, over time we have to change our prediction to understand that they will not be next to us on any day in the future. But those are not the only predictions that we have to cope with. There's also a level of simple habit when we live with someone or when we have a relationship with someone. We predict when we will interact with them and in what way we will interact with them. So, for example, you're at the grocery store, and you pick up a soy milk because your daughter is lactose intolerant. It's not a conscious decision. It's just an automatic habit. But if your daughter just died, you may for some time pick up soy milk even though no one is drinking soy milk in your home any longer. So even at the level of habits, we have to constantly be confronted by all the changes caused by the loss of this important person in our life.

Q: How is the presence of a loved one hardwired in the brain?

A: I would say they are not hardwired into our brain; rather they are in the wiring of our brain. So when we fall in love with our baby or we fall in love with the person who becomes our spouse, it changes the wiring. It updates the physical connections between neurons, and it changes the way that proteins are folded. The epigenetics [environmental and behavioral influences on the ways in which genes are expressed as proteins] of our brain change because we have fallen in love with this specific person.

Those physical traces in the brain have to be changed to reflect an updated understanding of the world, and that takes time. But it also takes experience. We have to have many, many days of being in the world without our spouse or our child or our best friend for the brain to create new connections and a new understanding of what it means to be without this person.

The general principle that this is how the brain works comes from Nobel Prize winners Edvard I. Moser and May-Britt Moser, who discovered what they call "object-trace cells" in the brain. They did experiments where they would take a rat and put it in a little black box every day. And then one day there was a blue tower inside the black box. The rat went to visit it, and because they were measuring single neurons firing, they could see that there were specific cells, [called object cells], that were firing as the rat investigated this little blue tower. And one day they took the blue tower away. For many days, even in the absence of the blue tower, [other cells that evidently tracked absence, the] object-trace cells, continued to fire because the rat expected that there would be a blue tower.

What's amazing about this, of course, is that a blue tower is not very important in the life of a rat. Think how much more important our loved ones are in our life and how many more ways they influence us. We can't do single recordings of single human neurons, but the general principle can be applied to grieving. We have to change the way our our neural networks are firing to understand our new reality.

Q: What role does closeness play? The closer we are to a person, the more, of course, the loss hurts.

A: It seems that "closeness" is a dimension we use to predict what our interaction will be like with a loved one when we see them. In the same way that we can predict the time and place we will see our loved one, we can also predict the closeness we will feel with them. If I said to you, for example, "Where is your partner?" or "Where is your child?" you probably would be able to give me almost an immediate answer. Those dimensions of time and space are a way that we keep our loved one's presence in our mind. In a similar way, we keep a sense of how close we are to them in our subconscious mind.

So, for example, we will often think of them when we're doing something stressful as a way to soothe ourselves, even if they're not present for us in that time and space. Just thinking about our closeness with them changes our stress response. Just as our brain cannot really understand the abstract idea that our loved one is no longer in time and space, it continues to expect our loved ones to respond to us. The fact that they don't respond to us ... in an illogical way, can feel like they're ignoring us. So I think people who are grieving too often feel overwhelmed with anger with this person for dying, and they know that is completely illogical. But the feeling is that if we are close to them, they should be responding to us.

When we're grieving, the feelings we have, the thoughts that we have, even some of the things that we do—we feel like we're losing our mind. But if you understand why your brain might be reacting this way, I think it gives us a little patience with ourselves. Grieving is a form of learning. And learning takes time and experience, and our brain is doing its best to help us. But it's going to take some time.

Q: You did the first neuroimaging study of grief in 2003. What did you find out?

A: When I began studying the psychology and neuroscience of grief, the primary way that researchers were thinking about the loss of a loved one was in a stress framework, the idea being that this is an incredibly stressful life event, and we respond to that stressful life event by coping with it. It was very much this idea of "you have so many things to cope with. And here is another thing on your plate that you have to cope with."

Because of some of the research I've done, we discovered that when we have a bonded relationship, it is encoded in the reward network of the brain. The reward network is motivating us to seek loved ones out and to enjoy them as we did when we were with them. That is how researchers now think about grief—as having had something taken away from us, from our sense of self, rather than having something added onto our plate. And this is a pretty big difference in thinking about how grieving works.

When people say, "I feel like part of myself is missing," this may not be only a metaphor. It may in fact be part of how the brain has encoded that relationship, so the absence of that person is like an amputation rather than simply an additional stressor.

Q: People usually say that time will heal all wounds. Is this also true for grief?

A: Yes but with caveats. Grieving can be thought of as a form of learning–learning that this person is really gone, learning to predict their absence, learning what it means to be a person who has grief or to understand our own identity as a widow instead of a married person, for example. Then it requires not only time but experience. So, for example, if you were in a coma for a month after a loved one had died, and you woke up to hear the news, you would be having the same grief reaction as before the coma. It's not time specifically that helps us to adapt; it's about having new experiences in the world and allowing our brain to understand what life is like now.

Because it is often very painful to be in the world, to see old friends or to go to a place where you spent time with the loved one, we often avoid those experiences. But in many ways, those are exactly the experiences that our brain needs to learn how to understand the world now. And so in psychotherapy, often we enable a grieving person to tackle some of these things they've been avoiding so they can learn new skills–how to allow a wave of grief to come but to also allow that wave to recede so they can continue to do meaningful things in life or to have relationships with living loved ones.

Q: What are the typical emotions people will experience, and where do they come from?

A: We have a much wider range of emotions than any of us expect when we are grieving. They include, of course, sadness and yearning. But they also include anger and blame and guilt and other things as well, such as panic. When we are separated from a loved one, we feel panicky. If you're in the grocery store, and you look down, and your toddler is not next to you, you feel this panic. People who are grieving often describe a sense of panic as well, because we expect our loved one to be there, and our natural response to their absence can be to feel panicky.

But grief is not only an emotional response. We have a physiological response as well. Our heart rate usually goes up a little bit. Our cortisol stress hormones increase, and these often make it difficult to eat or to sleep. All these changes can make us very off-balance, can make it difficult to concentrate or to remember important details in our day-to-day life.

Q: Is grief only about the loss of a loved one, or can it also come from other losses?

A: Where do we start? We know that for social mammals, attachment bonds are as vital as food and water to our survival. Because you are a human adult, I know that you had an attachment relationship that enabled you to survive to adulthood, which required you to be bonded with someone who cared for you. It is for this reason, I think, that our brain evolved mechanisms to create attachment bonds and to adapt when those bonds are broken. And obviously the most concrete example of breaking those bonds is through the death of a loved one.

But human relationships are broken for many reasons, whether that is a divorce or the "empty nest" when our children move out into the world or simply becoming estranged from a very close friend. These breaks change that bonded relationship so that we can no longer rely on the belief "I will always be there for you, and you will always be there for me." And so, I think, we experience these other disruptions in relationships as grief as well.

And grief is not only about the loss of a person. We have grief over the loss of many things–the loss of health, the loss of a job. Our brain might have evolved to understand the loss of a relationship as grief, but it's always also a loss of a part of ourselves. Even the language we use is helpful here. I describe myself as a daughter–that's a word that I use about me. When I lose a parent, it is a loss of an aspect of myself. Similarly, the loss of eyesight is the loss of how I function in the world with my eyes.

In a study some years ago, we found that the severity of yearning was greatest with bereavement and somewhat less with a breakup, but they were still the same qualitative experience. Of course, there are other things that impact breakups. If the other person initiated it, the yearning was much greater than if the griever had initiated or if it had been a mutual decision. Grief operates differently in these different types of losses but shares a common experience.

Q: Some people have a much harder time coping with the loss. Why is that?

A: We know from really detailed studies that although there are similarities across the way people grieve, not everyone has the same experience in grieving. For most of us, the waves of grief become less intense and less frequent over time. But for perhaps one in 10 bereaved people or even fewer, for many, many months, they don't show any change in their grief reaction. They still seem to be responding the same way they did right after the death happened.

We call this state prolonged grief. Most people continue to feel waves of grief for years after the loss of someone important, but typically their grieving starts to change within a year. For a few people, there is no change. It's important to identify them because psychotherapy can help them overcome some of these barriers that are preventing them from adapting.

There are some predictors for prolonged grief, and they include things such as preexisting mental health difficulties and having very little social support. Being very isolated also seems to predict poorer outcomes in grieving. We have a lot to learn about what individual variation in the brain leads to prolonged grieving, but the science is very much in its infancy.

Q: People who lost somebody will often, out of nowhere, have thoughts about the person. Where do they come from, and are they good or bad?

A: People are often very shocked by the intensity and frequency of these intrusive thoughts. There are a few things to know that can help you to feel more normal in the midst of these thoughts. One is that we actually have intrusive thoughts all the time. Another thing is that when a loved one is alive, thoughts about them just pop into our head. Our mind sends us push notifications like "don't forget that you have to pick up your daughter at sports and not at school today."

It's just that after they've died, the same intrusive thoughts are very distressing to us. The context in which they're happening is very different now and very painful. Intrusive thoughts can also lead us to ruminating–we keep going over it and over it, and we can't seem to let it go. One of the really common experiences that people have, a very natural and normal response, is the "could" or "should" thoughts. These are the million stories that we play out in our head where something could have gone differently. We should have gotten them to the hospital sooner or to the doctor.

For many grieving people, these stories go around and around and around in their head. And the challenge is that our brain can come up with an infinite number of these alternatives in which, if something was done at the right time, "my loved one would have lived." But the only reality that we are currently dealing with is the fact that they did not live. These thoughts are quite natural and normal and common, but they don't help us to adapt to what's happening now. Many people come to realize that there is no way through these thoughts; rather they have to find a way *around* the thoughts and allow them to recede.

Q: How does understanding the neuroscience of grief help people navigate this lonely landscape?

A: Neuroscience can give us some insight into why we feel such pain and how and why the brain is making that happen. I think it can make us feel more normal that our brain is on a learning trajectory. And we simply have to accept that things will be difficult for some time while our brain tries to update its understanding of the world. But it's also very comforting to understand how. When we have this loving relationship with someone, it means that our brain is permanently, physically changed. What that means is even after a loved one has died, they are still physically with us. They are still in those folded proteins and neural connections. And there's something, to me, very comforting about knowing that my mother or my father still lives in me physically.

This article originally appeared in Spektrum der Wissenschaft *and was reproduced with permission.*

About the Author

Claudia Christine Wolf is a science journalist and an editor at Spektrum der Wissenschaft, Scientific American*'s German-language sibling publication, where she covers psychology, biology and neuroscience.*

Shades of Grief: When Does Mourning Become a Mental Illness?

By Virginia Hughes

Sooner or later most of us suffer deep grief over the death of someone we love. The experience often causes people to question their sanity—as when they momentarily think they have caught sight of their loved one on a crowded street. Many mourners ponder, even if only abstractedly, their reason for living. But when are these disturbing thoughts and emotions normal—that is to say, they become less consuming and intense with the passage of time—and when do they cross the line to pathology, requiring ongoing treatment with powerful antidepressants or psychotherapy, or both?

Two proposed changes in the "bible" of psychiatric disorders—the *Diagnostic and Statistical Manual of Mental Disorders* (*DSM*)—aim to answer that question when the book's fifth edition comes out in 2013. One change expected to appear in the *DSM-5* reflects a growing consensus in the mental health field; the other has provoked great controversy.

In the less controversial change, the manual would add a new category: Complicated Grief Disorder, also known as traumatic or prolonged grief. The new diagnosis refers to a situation in which many of grief's common symptoms—such as powerful pining for the deceased, great difficulty moving on, a sense that life is meaningless, and bitterness or anger about the loss—last longer than six months. The controversial change focuses on the other end of the time spectrum: it allows medical treatment for depression in the first few weeks after a death. Currently the *DSM* specifically bars a bereaved person from being diagnosed with full-blown depression until at least two months have elapsed from the start of mourning.

Those changes matter to patients and mental health professionals because the manual's definitions of mental illness determine how people are treated and, in many cases, whether the therapy is paid for by insurance. The logic behind the proposed revisions, therefore, merits a further look.

Abnormal Grief

The concept of pathological mourning has been around since Sigmund Freud, but it began receiving formal attention more recently. In several studies of widows with severe, long-lasting grief in the 1980s and 1990s, researchers noticed that antidepressant medications relieved such depressive feelings as sadness and worthlessness but did nothing for other aspects of grief, such as pining and intrusive thoughts about the deceased. The finding suggested that complicated grief and depression arise from different circuits in the brain, but the work was not far enough along to make it into the current, fourth edition of the *DSM*, published in 1994. In the 886-page book, bereavement is relegated to just one paragraph and is described as a symptom that "may be a focus of clinical attention." Complicated grief is not mentioned.

Over the next few years other studies revealed that persistent, consuming grief may, in and of itself, increase the risk of other illnesses, such as heart problems, high blood pressure and cancer. Holly G. Prigerson, one of the pioneers of grief research, organized a meeting of loss experts in Pittsburgh in 1997 to hash out preliminary criteria for what she and her colleagues saw as an emerging condition, which they termed traumatic grief. Their view of its defining features: an intense daily yearning and preoccupation with the deceased. In essence, it is the inability to adjust to life without that person, notes Mardi J. Horowitz, professor of psychiatry at the University of California, San Francisco, and another early researcher of the condition. Prigerson, then an assistant professor at the Western Psychiatric Institute and Clinic in Pittsburgh, hoped the meeting would begin the process of finding enough evidence to support changing the *DSM*. "We knew that grief predicted a lot of bad outcomes–over and above depression and anxiety–and thought it was worthy of clinical attention in its own right," says Prigerson, now a professor of psychiatry at Harvard Medical School.

A spate of studies since then–not only of widows but of parents who had lost a child, tsunami survivors and others–has further confirmed and refined that initial description. In 2008 researchers got their first hint of what complicated grief disorder looks like at the neurological level. Mary-Frances O'Connor of U.C.L.A. scanned the brains of women who had lost their mother or a sister to cancer within the past five years. She compared the results of women who had displayed typical grief with those suffering from prolonged, unabated mourning. When, while inside the scanner, the study participants looked at images of the deceased or words associated with the death, both groups showed a burst of activity in neurological circuits known to be involved in pain. The women with prolonged grief, however, also showed a unique neural signature: increased activity in a nub of tissue called the nucleus accumbens. This area, part of the brain's reward center, also lights up on imaging scans when addicts look at photographs of drug paraphernalia and when mothers see pictures of their newborn infant. That does not mean that the women were addicted to their feelings of grief but rather that they still felt actively attached to the deceased. Meanwhile clinical studies have shown that a combination of cognitive therapy approaches used to treat major depression and post-traumatic stress may help some people with complicated grief work through it.

As these and other studies began to pile up, a few researchers turned to complex statistical analysis to validate more precisely the exact combination of features that define the condition. In 2009, more than 10 years after the Pittsburgh panel, Prigerson published data collected from nearly 300 grievers she had followed for more than two years. By analyzing which of some two dozen psychological symptoms tend to cluster together in these participants, she devised the criteria for complicated grief: the mandatory presence of daily yearning plus five out of nine other symptoms for longer than six months after a death. This is exactly the type of rigorous, quantitative study that is needed before a condition makes it into the *DSM*. "People who meet the criteria for complicated grief do not necessarily meet criteria for either depression or post-traumatic stress disorder," says Katherine Shear, a professor of psychiatry at Columbia University. "If you didn't have this disorder [in the *DSM*], then those people would not get treatment at all."

Controversial Treatment

The case for diagnosing people as depressed and treating them accordingly when they are still newly bereaved is more contentious. Although some symptoms of grief and depression overlap (sadness, insomnia), the two conditions are thought to be distinct. Grief is tied to a particular event, for example, whereas the origins of a bout of clinical depression are often more obscure. Antidepressants do not ease the longing for the deceased that grievers feel. So in most cases, treating grieving people for depression is ineffective.

A few studies, however, have suggested that mourning may trigger depression in the same way that other major stresses—such as being raped or losing one's job—can bring about the condition. If so, some people who grieve may also be clinically depressed. It seems unfair, advocates of changing the *DSM* argue, to make mourners wait so long for medical help when anyone else can be treated for depression after just two weeks of consistent depression. "On the basis of scientific evidence, they're just like anybody else with depression," says Kenneth S. Kendler, a member of the *DSM-5* Mood Disorder Work Group, which reviews all proposed changes to the manual related to anxiety, depression and bipolar disorder (a condition characterized by extreme mood swings). It is for this reason that the group recently suggested deleting the clause that specifies a two-month wait before mourners can receive a diagnosis of, and therefore treatment for, depression.

Critics of the move counter that it will lead to unwarranted diagnoses and overtreatment. "It's a disastrous and foolish idea," says Allen Frances, who chaired the task force that produced the fourth edition of the *DSM*. He worries about how the *DSM-5* may be used by sales representatives from pharmaceutical companies to urge doctors to write more prescriptions. Indeed, Frances believes that changes in the edition that he oversaw inadvertently sparked an unwarranted explosion of diagnoses for bipolar disorder in children. Prigerson, for her part, predicts a general backlash against the idea that mourners might ever need psychiatric treatment. "There will be vitriolic debates when the public fully appreciates the fact that the *DSM* is pathologizing the death of a loved one within two weeks," she says.

In many ways, parsing the differences between normal grief, complicated grief and depression reflects the fundamental dilemma of psychiatry: mental disorders are diagnosed using subjective criteria and are usually an extension of a normal state. So any definition of where normal ends and abnormal begins will be the object of strongly held opinions. As Frances says, "There is no bright line–it is always going to be a matter of judgment."

Election Grief Is Real. Here's How to Cope

By Meghan Bartels

An impassioned election has come to an end, but the emotions of the past few months have not. One of the emotions a lot of people are experiencing is grief, more often associated with death than the voting process. *Scientific American* spoke with Pauline Boss, an emeritus professor at the University of Minnesota, who spent 45 years as a psychotherapist. She coined the term "ambiguous loss" in her work with wives of soldiers missing in action in the 1970s; more recently, she has applied the idea to what people around the world have experienced during the COVID pandemic.

[An edited transcript of the interview follows.]

Q: What is grief?

A: Grief is simply the outcome of loss, but there's a caveat–the criterion for what you lost is that you were attached to it.

You can grieve things that are both clear and unclear. Most of our literature is based on a clear loss–death or the loss of money, things that can be quantified or proven. But there are many, many kinds of losses that remain ambiguous. It's a term I came up with in the late 1970s that apparently gave a name to a kind of loss that heretofore went unacknowledged. People felt sad; they felt like they wanted to grieve, but nobody would come to their house to comfort them; there were no religious rituals for this kind of loss. There just was no acknowledgment of it.

Now we know there is such a thing as ambiguous loss, and I think that's what people might be experiencing now

During the COVID pandemic, for example, we had loss of trust in the world as a safe place because of the virus. Many of us baked bread because that was a couple hours of being in control again and having a good outcome. It was certainty, two hours of certainty–that, by the way, is a good way to cope with a situation you can't control.

Now we have a kind of loss that I think is causing some grief for people who wanted a different outcome of this election. It's really quite important to understand the feeling. It is a normal response if you're in the midst of something you didn't expect and you don't like, and it came suddenly, unexpectedly. It's a major loss.

Q: Do we need to change the way we think about emotions such as sadness and anger?

A: We should normalize the anger and the sadness. I think we jump too quickly to pathologize emotions that are scary. I think you need to be patient with yourself if you're feeling angry, sad, grieving right now. I think that's a normal reaction to a surprising outcome and an outcome that, in our view, is going backward and not forward.

So accept your feelings. Know there's no closure to grief. Know you had a loss. List your losses–I would recommend people actually write them down.

Q: What are some of the psychological losses people might be feeling after the election?

A: The loss of hopes and dreams and plans that they thought were coming from the other candidate; a loss of certainty in the future that was what they wanted; loss of trust in the world as a safe place; loss of feelings of freedom over your own body; the loss of support for people who have lesser means than the rest of us do; the loss of support for your neighbor and people who are different from you–it's a grief that remains unresolved.

It's not like a grief of a person for whom you have a death certificate and a funeral after and rituals of support and comfort. We're stuck with this. I wrote about it as frozen grief.

Q: What is it that freezes that grief?

A: A lack of proof—a lack of certainty that you have lost something, because you can't see it. If someone died, you can see the body or the ashes; you can see the death certificate. There's something official that says this person you loved and were attached to is now gone, and while that is very sad, you at least have certainty.

With a more abstract kind of loss, there is no proof that you have lost trust in the world except your perception. And if you perceive it to be true, it is true for you—that you're feeling helpless or powerless that things didn't go your way.

With frozen grief, you could be immobilized. That's the danger. Don't be immobilized. You need to do something active in order to deal with a situation you can't control. Be active in your neighborhoods at the grassroots level. It will help to be active, not just to sit back and grumble and not just to lash out either. Action is psychologically what helps when you're feeling helpless.

Q: That sounds like maybe a long-term strategy. You talked about the example of baking bread; would that be a sort of short-term strategy for managing this type of grief?

A: Absolutely. Short term, you have to do something you can control when you're in a situation you can't control. Do something you can control—in your house, in your home, with your family. Go running, listen to music, go to a movie, do something that requires action, that makes your body move. You'll feel better for that. Go see a neighbor.

Long term, get involved. Get involved with whatever works for change that will bring us closer to the future, not take us backward.

Q: Do you have any words of wisdom for sort of how people can make space for grief over time?

A: It doesn't go away. Grief sort of turns itself into sadness, but don't expect it to ever go away. You may even shed a tear or have an emotion of sadness 20 years from now if you remember this time—and that's normal. That is normal grief. You do not have to find closure. If you were attached to some thing, some person, some idea, and you lost it, you will carry a sadness about that forever. You will remember it. You won't forget it, nor should you have to.

When people say to you, "Aren't you over it yet?" please respond to them and say, the current knowledge is that you don't have to get over loss and grief. You learn to live with it, and you learn to live with loss by finding a new purpose in it, finding something you can do to change things. You have to find a purpose in your loss, and that purpose should be something active.

Q: I could see someone feeling really cynical and sad saying, like, "If losing things you're attached to causes grief, then I'm just not going to be attached to things." Is that actually a healthy response?

A: No. I'm using attachment rather loosely. In psychology it has a narrower definition, but it is a motivation for our actions and our beliefs and values.

Q: So attachments are really important, even if they do cause you pain sometimes?

A: That's right. It's a good time to sit and reflect on your own life and your own attachments. What do you care about? What do you care about in your own body? What do you care about in your own family, in your neighborhood, in your nation and in the world? I care about climate change not because it will matter in my life so much anymore, given my age, but because I care about my grandchildren and their children.

Q: Is it possible to cultivate more resilience to this kind of grief in the future?

A: Yes. Increase your tolerance for ambiguity and keep increasing your tolerance for uncertainty. We hate uncertainty in this culture.

There is, in fact, a tolerance for ambiguity scale. It was born out of a scale now called the authoritarian personality scale. [*Editor's Note: That scale was originally developed in the aftermath of World War II by philosopher Theodor Adorno as a response to Nazism. A higher tolerance for ambiguity is related to lower susceptibility to fascist ideologies.*]

Change is necessary. If a system of human beings doesn't change, they die. And right now I think we're on the precipice of not wanting to change, and that's not a good thing. That's going backward. I think we should work toward bringing about change now at the community level, wherever you have power and agency, whatever level you have it at. Maybe it's just in your family, maybe it's just in yourself, or maybe it is in your community or state or nation or globally. But work for change—because change is the one thing that will keep us going.

Q: Are there any strategies that people can use to cultivate that tolerance for ambiguity and uncertainty in themselves?

A: Yes. Go see some improvisation at the theater. Go to listen to some jazz music, which is totally improvisation. Do something different that you've never done before. Learn a new language; go travel in a foreign country alone. Get to know some people you never knew before that are unlike yourself. Stretch yourself; reach out; do something different. Take a hike on a new path.

I'm not against certainty. I want my accountant to think in binary. And in our sports world, you either win or you lose. That's a binary. But in human relationships and in our human condition, the binary does not work so well. We're often in that shadowland of ambiguity and uncertainty.

Q: Is there anything else you want to say about grief people might be feeling right now?

A: Don't be afraid of it. Just know that it's a normal reaction to an outcome you didn't want or expect. And it doesn't need to go away, but hopefully it doesn't immobilize you. The grief is frozen; you yourself shouldn't be.

About the Author

Meghan Bartels is a science journalist based in New York City. She joined Scientific American *in 2023 and is now a senior news reporter there. Previously, she spent more than four years as a writer and editor at Space.com, as well as nearly a year as a science reporter at Newsweek, where she focused on space and Earth science. Her writing has also appeared in* Audubon, Nautilus, Astronomy *and* Smithsonian, *among other publications. She attended Georgetown University and earned a master's degree in journalism at New York University's Science, Health and Environmental Reporting Program.*

Section 3: Emotions and the Environment

Summertime Sadness Could Be a Type of Seasonal Affective Disorder

By Lauren Leffer

Has the heat got you down? You're probably not alone.

Wintertime—with its long, dark nights—is the season most associated with low mood and depression. But sun-filled summer days can also bring on the doldrums, particularly for the subset of people who experience a summertime version of seasonal affective disorder (SAD)—a type of depression with a periodic pattern. Those with a lesser-known and lesser-studied summer SAD variant may feel "out of sync with the rest of the world" because they experience depression just as summer breaks and pool party invites pick up, says Thomas Wehr, a psychiatrist and scientist emeritus at the National Institutes of Health.

Depression can occur any time of year, but some research indicates that the warmer months can be particularly challenging for certain people. A growing number of studies indicate links between body temperature and depression, and high outside temperatures have been linked to mood and mental health crises. The prevalence of summertime SAD remains unclear, but as climate change makes extreme weather more common, understanding the effects of hot days on mental health—and developing new, effective treatments—has higher stakes.

What is Summer SAD?

Wehr and his colleague Norman Rosenthal, a psychiatrist then at the NIH, coined the term SAD in the early 1980s based on their research into people with cyclical winter depression. After publication, they received some unexpected letters from people who vehemently attested to having the opposite condition: depression in the summer and improved mood in winter.

Wehr and Rosenthal's team investigated these accounts in a 1987 case report, which described 12 people who displayed a pattern of recurrent depressive episodes in the summertime. In a 1991 follow-up paper, they compared another 60 participants, half of whom seemed to have summer SAD and half of whom had winter SAD. Both groups met clinical criteria for depression that usually reoccurred seasonally, but the two cohorts experienced different symptoms.

Participants in the winter group "were very lethargic" and compared themselves to hibernating animals, says Rosenthal, who is now a professor at the Georgetown University School of Medicine. In contrast, the summer group was more "irritable" and "restless," he adds. The winter cohort more frequently slept, overate and experienced weight gain, whereas the summer cohort reported higher incidences of insomnia, reduced appetite and more frequent weight loss.

The prevalence of summer SAD "would be a complete guess" because of limited data, Rosenthal says. Based on his interactions with people who do have the condition, Wehr believes it may be more common in warmer and more humid locations and in regions with limited access to air-conditioning. But Rosenthal and Wehr say much more work is needed to truly understand how common summer SAD is and where it most frequently occurs.

Compared with the winter variant, "the literature on summer SAD is much smaller," says Kelly Rohan, a clinical psychologist who studies subtypes of recurrent depression at the University of Vermont. Both the 1987 and 1991 studies had a small sample size, and there has been minimal follow-up work. Nevertheless, Rohan says those early case studies are robust and convincing because they thoroughly examine and describe peoples' symptoms.

Much research has linked winter SAD to shorter daylight hours and reduced sunlight exposure, causing clinicians to suggest light therapy as a potential treatment. In contrast, Rohan says, the primary triggers for the summer type are assumed to be heat and humidity.

Some researchers question whether SAD–either the summer or winter variety–should be a medically recognized condition altogether. "As it's conceptualized, I am skeptical," says Steven Lobello, a psychology professor at Auburn University at Montgomery. In 2016 Lobello and his colleagues published a study involving survey data from 34,000 people in the U.S. that found no population-level indication that depressive episodes were more common in the winter. A 2019 review found "some support for seasonal variation in clinical depression" but noted that prior research was "fragmented," with varied findings.

Multiple studies have documented that heat can affect mood disorders and behavior, says Kim Meidenbauer, an assistant professor of psychology at Washington State University, who studies heat's psychological effects. Increases in aggression and violent crimes have been well documented on hotter days and during summertime, Meidenbauer says. Recent studies have also found that psychiatric emergency room visits for depression and other mental health disorders peak on hotter days, mood trends more negative with increased heat and suicide rates rise in conjunction with temperature. The latter study on suicide risk, which was published in 2018, also found a decline in well-being corresponding to hotter outdoor temperatures, according to an accompanying analysis of depressive language in 600 million posts on Twitter (now X) between May 2014 and July 2015.

Rosenthal notes the findings about psychiatric hospital admissions, suicide risk and even online activity are in line with his previous work on SAD, which also concluded that people who face mental health struggles in the summer are more agitated than those who do so in the winter. People who are depressed but restless–with energy to spare–might be more likely to act on suicidal urges or end up in the hospital or, he explains.

Meidenbauer notes there are a few hypotheses for why heat might trigger depression. For one, "it interrupts your sleep," she says–and quality shut-eye is critical for mental health. Maintaining a normal body temperature is also a resource-intensive process, Meidenbauer says. Heat can become a physical stressor, particularly for children, older people and those taking certain medications that disrupt the body's ability to cool down. If people are uncomfortable over a long period of time, that invariably affects emotional state, she says.

One 2018 review study indicates that heat may also disrupt neurotransmitters involved in brain activity while we're awake, which could contribute to depression. In addition, multiple studies have found that depressed people have an elevated body temperature, especially at night, which suggests depression itself may undermine the body's ability to regulate temperature.

Wehr says investigating the relationship between temperature and mental health could help home in on the mechanisms underlying depression and even improve treatments, which is especially important because experts overwhelmingly agree that climate change is likely to exacerbate the mental health risks of hot weather.

Summer SAD Solutions

Treatments for summer depression are understudied, Rohan says. There is some evidence that lowering the body temperature via air-conditioning, cold showers or swimming sessions can help at least temporarily. In Rosenthal and Wehr's first case report, one patient's mood improved when Wehr recommended she try confining herself to an air-conditioned house and regularly taking cold showers, but she reported feeling depressed again just nine days after stopping this regimen.

Meidenbauer points out that staying indoors in heavily air-conditioned spaces and taking frequent cold showers likely isn't sustainable from an environmental, practical or financial perspective. Swamp coolers and fans may be cheaper, more accessible options—particularly for that extra critical nighttime cooling.

Counterintuitively, exposure to high heat via saunas and hot tubs might offer longer-term relief. Some clinical trials have found that peoples' depression improved when treated with hot baths. This could be because short-duration, high-intensity heat resets dormant or dysfunctional thermoregulatory systems in people with depression, says Ashley Mason, a clinical psychologist and an associate professor at the University of California, San Francisco. If people with summer SAD have thermoregulation issues, Mason suggests, such heat therapies may be especially helpful.

Beyond manipulating body temperature, simply tracking mood and comfort level throughout the summer season can be useful, Meidenbauer says. Noticing a pattern is the first step toward changing it, she adds. If you know that heat dampens your mood, that's one more tool you can use to potentially predict, prepare for and mitigate (metaphorically) dark days. Rosenthal agrees. "Look at the things that make you feel better and do them more. And look at the things that make you feel worse and do them less," he says. This tip can help people who experience mental health issues any time of year.

If you or someone you know is struggling or having thoughts of suicide, help is available. Call or text the 988 Suicide & Crisis Lifeline at 988 or use the online Lifeline Chat.

About the Author

Lauren Leffer is a contributing writer and former tech reporting fellow at Scientific American. *She covers many subjects, including artificial intelligence, climate and weird biology, because she's curious to a fault. Follow her on X @lauren_leffer and on Bluesky: @laurenleffer.bsky.social*

Fact or Fiction?: "Spring Fever" Is a Real Phenomenon

By Christie Nicholson

There's an illness that has been documented by poets for centuries. Its symptoms include a flushed face, increased heart rate, appetite loss, restlessness and daydreaming. It's spring fever, that wonderfully amorphous disease we all recognize come April and May.

"Spring fever is not a definitive diagnostic category," says Michael Terman, director of the Center for Light Treatment and Biological Rhythms at Columbia University Medical Center. "But I would say it begins as a rapid and yet unpredictable fluctuating mood and energy state that contrasts with the relative low [of the] winter months that precede it."

Such spring fever remains a fuzzy medical category, but there has been a great deal of research on how seasonal changes affect our mood and behavior. Matthew Keller, postdoctoral fellow at the Virginia Institute for Psychiatric and Behavioral Genetics in Richmond, studied 500 people in the U.S. and Canada and found that the more time people spent outside on a sunny spring day the better their mood. Such good moods decreased during the hotter summer months and there is an optimal temperature for them, Keller claims: 72 degrees Fahrenheit, otherwise known as room temperature.

Of course, spring doesn't just lighten our mood; as Alfred Lord Tennyson described, "In the spring a young man's fancy lightly turns to thoughts of love." Studies show that sexual behavior in mammals follows a seasonal pattern, one that promotes survival. In fact, researchers discovered that birth spikes in field mice are more significant the farther the mice are from the equator, as seasons become more pronounced. The same trend was also seen in hares and deer, according to *Mammalian Reproductive Biology* by biologist

Frank Bronson of the University of Texas. It is well documented that animals and humans track seasons by measuring the length of days through an internal biological clock, and this is what controls their breeding.

The biological clock, called the suprachiasmatic nucleus (SCN), sits in mammals' hypothalamus. It monitors light through a pathway to the retina and conveys information about day length to the pineal gland. This pea-size gland, tucked at the base of the cerebrum, controls the secretion of melatonin, dubbed the sleep hormone because it is only released in the dark or in dim light. The duration of melatonin release changes with nocturnal length, which is longest during winter. And it has been thought that our increased energy in the spring months is somehow linked to the decreased duration of melatonin production, due to shorter nights.

"From a biological perspective, most types of animals, and maybe even plants, have seasonal variation in behavior and physiology; there are seasonal cycles in human rates of conception," says Thomas Wehr of the National Institute of Mental Health, who reviewed the effect of biological rhythms on reproduction in 2001 for the *Journal of Biological Rhythms*. Historically there have been more births in the spring. In the late 16th century birth rates typically spiked to 20 percent above the average in March—meaning the babies were conceived in June—but over the past 400 years rates have flattened to about 10 percent above the average, according to research done by David Lam at the University of Michigan's Population Studies Center in Ann Arbor.

Cultural and social factors influence conception patterns but biology plays a strong role, as shown by peaks that are 20 percent above average during June—technically the tail end of spring—in the production of reproductive fuel: luteinizing hormone, which produces testosterone in men and triggers ovulation in women. Research also shows that successful in vitro fertilization follows the same seasonal peaks as natural birth. "In humans we don't know for sure what the causal connection is," Wehr says, "but if most other mammals are using changes in day length, then the melatonin signal and conception rates is a pretty plausible relationship, but more research is needed."

The idea that melatonin triggers our mood change in the spring is "too convenient an explanation," Terman counters. "Melatonin is more like the hands of the clock, it's not the essential variable." Since the mid-1980s researchers have focused on the seasonal effect on moods, with the emergence of a diagnostic label for winter depression, seasonal affective disorder (SAD). No one knows the exact cause of SAD, Terman says, but there are distinct patterns of winter depression lifting in the spring. And the key for that rise in mood, he argues, is the earlier onset of morning light. He has shown that there is more depression on the western edges of time zones in the U.S., where the sun rises later.

Clearly, there are marked correlations between moods, behavior and the lengthening days of spring, but the precise cause for our renewed energy remains elusive. The evidence for spring fever remains largely anecdotal. But, just as SAD has proved sadly real, spring fever edges away from science fiction, even if it is not quite science fact.

How I Overcame Solastalgia

By Queen Essang

As I sit in my backyard in Abuja, Nigeria, looking out at the open landscape around me, I can't help but feel a deep sense of loss. The rolling hills that were once richly carpeted with wild ferns, daisies, lupines and goldenrods are now dotted with invasive species that have choked out the native flora. The river that was once crystal clear, reflecting the azure sky and teeming with darting fish as dragonflies glided by, is now muddied by sediments and pollutants from nearby construction and agriculture.

This feeling of loss and dislocation, a combination of nostalgia for what once was and profound sadness for what has been irretrievably altered, has a name: solastalgia. Coined by philosopher Glenn Albrecht, it is the emotional distress caused by environmental change, particularly when it affects the place we call home. Essentially it is the feeling of being homesick while at home.

Despite the pain of this feeling, there is hope. Solastalgia has inspired me. It serves as a strong motivator to push for the protection and rejuvenation of our environments. It reminds us of the intrinsic value of nature and the importance of stewardship. When we acknowledge our grief and channel it into positive action, we empower ourselves to fight for the landscapes we love and to safeguard biodiversity, transforming our sorrow into tangible steps for change. Our bonds with nature are resilient and worth nurturing for future generations.

Growing up, I spent countless hours in the woods behind my childhood home surrounded by majestic oaks with their sprawling canopies, towering pines reaching for the heavens, and graceful willows swaying gently by the river's edge. I would often find myself in the embrace of the ancient pines, their earthy scent grounding me as I wandered underneath their branches. The woods were my sanctuary. Each tree had a story, a memory attached to it. I remember the laughter of friends echoing throughout the canopy as we played hide-and-seek, the sun filtering through the foliage, casting dappled shadows on the forest floor, and the quiet moments spent sitting up against a tree trunk, feeling at one with nature.

When I returned home after five years in college, I was struck by how much the ecosystem had changed. As climate change accelerates and development encroaches on familiar spaces, I find myself grappling with an unsettling reality. The vibrant tapestry of my childhood is unraveling. In its place lies a landscape marked by change–change that feels invasive and alien.

Today, in my backyard, I find myself thinking about the day years ago when I encountered a friendly female waterbuck while wandering through the lush Stubbs Creek reserve. The forest was alive with playful squirrels, and the occasional fox darted through the underbrush. Chirping robins and warblers and buzzing insects created a symphony that sounded like home. Now I realize many of those trees have been felled, replaced by sterile housing developments devoid of the forest's life and character.

Nestled within this vibrant landscape was Ibeno Lake. I had taken pride in its clear water, where families of ducks and geese often swam gracefully by. The lake was joy: a place for summer swims, lazy afternoons spent floating on rafts, evenings filled with the laughter of friends gathered around bonfires. It was here that I learned the rhythm of nature. Now I watch in dismay as algae blooms choke the water, turning it a murky green.

The emotional turmoil is not mine alone; it resonates with many people who are witnessing similar transformations in their environments. The deep sense of solastalgia manifests as a grief that is often overlooked–a sorrow not for a person but for a place. It is a longing for a connection that feels increasingly out of reach as the landscapes we once knew and loved are irrevocably altered.

Every time I see a familiar landmark disappear or a beloved habitat shrink, I can't help but reflect on how a once vivid collection of biodiversity is transforming into a homogenized landscape. This transformation induces a precarious tipping of nature's equilibrium. Climate change is a fundamental cause, but pollution from nearby industrial complexes has contributed significantly to the degradation of the natural environment. Deforestation spurred by the relentless pursuit of urban development continues to erode extensive forestland, and unsustainable extraction has stripped the land of its natural resources, leaving scars that are slow to heal.

I cannot stand idly by. I began to educate myself about conservation efforts shortly after I returned home, driven by the changes I witnessed in my environment. I have joined local conservation groups, participating in tree-planting initiatives to restore native species and combat the invasion of nonnative flora. I have also engaged in cleanup efforts at Ibeno Lake, rallying friends and family to help remove litter and debris from the shorelines so we can restore its natural beauty. Education is vital, too; I strive to raise awareness in my community about the importance of preserving our natural spaces.

In my conversations with family and friends, I find that solastalgia is a common experience. We often reminisce about the landscapes of our youth, remembering the places that influenced our lives. These discussions take on a somber tone as we realize our memories are becoming associated more with what we are losing than with what is left. The world is changing, and as a result, so are we.

As I reflect on my journey with solastalgia, I realize it is not merely a feeling of loss but also a call to reconnect. It urges us to find new ways to engage with our surroundings, to create memories in the face of change and to honor the beauty that still exists, despite the challenges. Although the landscape may shift, our appreciation for it can remain steadfast, reminding us that our bond with nature is resilient and worth nurturing for future generations.

In an era when environmental challenges loom large, solastalgia serves as a poignant reminder of what is at stake. It is an invitation to cherish our homes, to advocate for their protection and to cultivate a deep-rooted sense of responsibility for the world we inhabit. As we confront the realities of a changing climate, may we find solace not only in our memories but also in our collective capacity to foster a thriving future for both people and the planet, in a harmonious balance that nurtures the vibrant tapestry of life.

This is an opinion and analysis article, and the views expressed by the author or authors are not necessarily those of Scientific American.

About the Author

Queen Essang lives in the Federal Capital Territory (FCT), Abuja, Nigeria, and works as a freelance writer focusing on environmental issues and their psychological impact. She has a degree in botany and ecological studies from the University of Uyo in Akwa Ibom State, Nigeria, and was involved in the strategic implementation of climate change action and mitigation measures in the FCT administration's department of forestry.

I'll Bee There for You: Do Insects Feel Emotions?

By Jason G. Goldman

Charles Darwin once wrote in his book *The Expression of Emotions in Man and Animals* that insects "express anger, terror, jealousy and love." That was in 1872. Now, nearly 150 years later, researchers have discovered more evidence that Darwin might have been onto something. Bumblebees seem to have a "positive emotionlike state," according to a study published this week in *Science*. In other words, they may experience something akin to happiness. To some, the idea is still controversial, however.

Unlike humans, you can't simply ask a bee to interrogate its own emotions and describe them. Instead, researchers have to look for evidence that the insects have the cognitive, behavioral and physiological building blocks that, when combined, can give rise to a complex phenomenon like emotion.

Biologist Clint Perry of Queen Mary, University of London devised an experiment to do just that. He and his colleagues trained bumblebees to distinguish between a blue flower placed on the left side of a container and a green one on the right. When the bees explored the blue flower, they found a 30 percent sugar solution. But when they explored the green one, they slurped up plain, unsweetened water. Eventually, the bees learned to associate the blue flower with a tasty reward.

Then the researchers tested the bees on ambiguously colored flowers at intermediate locations. Half of the insects were given a 60 percent sugar solution prior to the test, and those bees flew faster toward the ambiguous blue-green flower. The remaining bees that were not given the sugar flew more slowly.

The assumption that an ambiguous stimulus contains a reward despite the lack of evidence is called an optimism bias. Perry's experiment suggests that a bit of sugar amped up the bees into a positive emotional state, making them more optimistic that the flower would contain a sugary treat.

Sound familiar? Something similar is true in humans—newborn infants cry less if they've been offered a sweet snack, and a bit of candy increases feelings of positivity and improves bad moods in adults, too. "Many of us view the world in a better way when we have a nice piece of dark chocolate," Perry says.

To be sure that the bees' flying behavior resulted from their underlying emotional state and was not simply a sugar high, the researchers tested the insects on other, unfamiliar flowers in new colors. The effect, Perry says, was specific to flowers with colors that fell somewhere between the blue and green hues they were trained on, not for any other color.

In another test involving a simulated predator attack, the sugar-addled bees showed the same optimism bias. In the wild, bumblebees are sometimes attacked by lurking crab spiders. To mimic such an attack, the researchers gently grabbed the bees with a sponge-tipped mechanical stamp for three seconds before releasing them. The insects that were given sugar water before the "attack" resumed foraging more rapidly than those that weren't, suggesting their positive emotions made them less cautious and more optimistic in this situation as well.

In a final experiment, when the researchers gave the bees a drug that disrupted receptors for dopamine, a neurotransmitter linked with motivation and reward, the bias disappeared, echoing the way this brain chemical works in mammals. "Many scientists, even entomologists, still believe that insects are genetically preprogrammed, rigid, behavioral machines," Perry says. University of Arizona entomologist Katy Prudic, who was not involved with the study, also disagrees with that idea. "Because they're built so differently, we tend to downplay their emotional states," she says—"probably because we don't see it in the same way we would with a dog or a cat or a cow."

There is no intrinsic reason that insects shouldn't experience emotions. Feelings, on the other hand, are a separate issue. Even though we use the two terms interchangeably in common parlance, scientists use them differently. "Emotions are collections of actions, and numerous species have emoted," says neuroscientist and philosopher Antonio Damasio of the University of Southern California, "though we can not be certain that they felt their emotings." In other words, emotions are the body's adaptive response to external events or stimuli. Feelings are the subjective experience of them.

So on receiving bad news, your blood pressure might spike and your respiration rate might plummet. If you saw a mountain lion while hiking, your heart and respiration rates would both increase, your brain would be flooded with cortisol and adrenaline, and your pupils would dilate. These are your body's emotional responses. And they can be, but are not necessarily, coupled with the subjective feelings of sadness or fear, respectively.

The same seems to go for bumblebees, although Perry did not demonstrate that bees have feelings. "We didn't show that they feel happy," he says. The evidence showed instead that bees possess the cognitive, behavioral and physiological mechanisms that underlie emotions.

"Feeling implies the presence of a mind and a mental experience, [or] consciousness," Damasio explains. "I have every reason to believe that invertebrates not only have emotions but also the possibility of feeling those emotions." If insects have feelings, it would have tremendous implications for the way we think about these creatures, including how we attempt to control them as pests.

For now, Perry hopes this research will simply encourage folks to see insects as more than just tiny, unthinking machines.

About the Author

Jason G. Goldman is a science journalist based in Los Angeles. He has written about animal behavior, wildlife biology, conservation, and ecology for Scientific American, Los Angeles *magazine, the* Washington Post, *the* Guardian, *the BBC,* Conservation *magazine, and elsewhere. He contributes to* Scientific American's

"60-Second Science" podcast, and is co-editor of Science Blogging: The Essential Guide *(Yale University Press). He enjoys sharing his wildlife knowledge on television and on the radio, and often speaks to the public about wildlife and science communication.*

Section 4: Controlling Your Emotions

Personality Can Change from One Hour to the Next

By Francine Russo

Psychologists use personality traits such as extroversion, neuroticism or anxiety as a means of characterizing typical patterns of thought, emotion and behavior that differ from one person to the next. From this perspective, the constituents of personality consist of a collection of relatively stable traits that are hard to change.

But the assumption that you can routinely measure these traits with questionnaires that identify typical behavior has come into question in the past two decades. The issue is not only that behavioral changes happen often but that they occur from day to day and hour to hour. Someone could be open and agreeable at noon but negative and rigid at two o'clock. Such oscillations in daily feelings and behavior–designated with the bland title of intraindividual variability, or IIV–are, in fact, so great they rival or even exceed differences in personality traits such as extroversion or conscientiousness that can be measured between one person and another.

The name for this field appeared in 2004 when Peter C. M. Molenaar, an emeritus professor of human development and psychology at Pennsylvania State University, championed IIV in a manifesto entitled "Bringing the Person Back into Scientific Psychology, This Time Forever." In it, he used a series of math and physics calculations to illustrate the degree of dynamic flux in personality while deriding standard methods of psychological testing.

This view of the importance of IIV has continued to gain popularity in the years since publication of Molenaar's manifesto. It has contributed to a better understanding of personality and led to changes in some forms of psychotherapy. Researchers have learned that variability in responses to stressful daily events–from having a fight with your spouse to getting stuck in traffic–can yield important insights about people's long-term emotional and physical health.

The research underlying this shift can be seen in a 20-year study of stress and health that also probed daily personality variability in more than 3,500 adults. Penn State developmental psychologist David Almeida and his colleagues asked subjects on eight consecutive days about stress levels and emotions throughout the previous 24 hours (and gathered a series of physiological measures). The list of people's stressors included arguments with a family member, work deadlines, an overload of home tasks and a retinue of ordinary daily hassles. Among the many emotions the researchers asked about were joy, anger, fear and anxiety. They also made queries about thoughts related to worry and behaviors such as physical activity and sleep. The investigators repeated this probe twice more at 10-year intervals. Almeida says they concluded that "daily experience–once deemed relatively unimportant to health–has both short- and long-term consequences on a variety of emotional, physical and cognitive outcomes."

Almeida's team calculated how much of what we typically think of as a personality trait actually is just that or can be understood as a passing emotion. "We see it in how grumpy people are," he says. "We think, 'Oh, this is a grumpy person.' In fact, half of their grumpiness is a personality trait, and half would be within the person's variability from day to day." He notes that people with positive traits such as openness or agreeability show only a 30 percent variation in traits such as quickness to anger or worry.

Some researchers have delved further in trying to determine how much one's immediate circumstances affect short-term psychological states. Stanford University professor of psychology and communication Nilam Ram has focused his work on how these hour-to-hour, day-to-day fluctuations are a response to the context in which they occur–such as at work, at home, while spending time with one's children or at the doctor's office. Until recently, high or low emotional variability had been seen as a personality trait in itself. Ram says, however, that these ups and downs can reflect the coming and going throughout the day of different aspects of an individual's personality or an immediate response to a person or event.

Take, for example, an individual participating in a study that gathers hourly reports of their emotions. Someone with high IIV might be considered an emotionally labile person. Or their emotional fluctuations might indicate that they are experiencing a series of unpredictable events in their life, perhaps arising from a chaotic workplace. In fact, Ram says, the emotional reports researchers receive from people they observe in their studies are probably a combination of some aspects of the immediate environment and elements of their personality—how reactive they are to what's around them and how well they regulate their emotions.

Stress in the moment differs depending on the kind of pressures exerted. Scientists have learned to measure and evaluate the impact of certain categories of stress. A fight with a spouse often results in more of an emotional upset than a work deadline, which, in turn, applies more pressure than daily hassles such as train delays or finding out the dog has pooped on the rug again.

Researchers typically measure IIV by assessing the same person at short intervals—such as every 24 hours for a week or five times each day—but psychologist Nadin Beckmann of Durham University in England and her colleagues adopted a different approach. The investigators asked each of the 288 working professionals in their study a series of questions about their personality—whether they were hardworking, contemplative, vulnerable, moody, and so on—at just one point in time and presented the same queries to up to five of each of the participants' family members, close friends or colleagues.

Momentary states, Beckmann explains, reflect how particular personality traits reveal themselves as a person responds to differing situations. We know intuitively that we do not think, feel and behave the same way at home as we do at work or while out socializing with friends. Beckmann's results show that intrapersonal variability fluctuates systematically by context regardless of which person is evaluating it. A person might be seen as more conscientious at work than at home and more extroverted with friends than with co-workers.

As researchers have learned to quantify this kind of hour-to-hour variability, they have started to evaluate what vicissitudes mean in devising a larger picture of personality. Ram says he might measure hourly fluctuations in a person's mood against monthly variations in self-esteem. If the person's mood changes a lot but their self-esteem remains relatively constant, one interpretation might be that their level of self-esteem is not much influenced by the temporary highs or lows they might experience from a compliment or a put-down.

In recent years Penn State research psychologist and cognitive-behavioral therapist Michelle Newman has found IIV invaluable both for performing research and for devising new ways to treat patients. In the days before smartphones, she says, patients in therapy or participants in a study would fill out a questionnaire that summarized their beliefs about themselves. They were asked to record hour-to-hour feelings with pen and paper or on an electronic note-taking device such as a PalmPilot. Finding these tasks cumbersome, they'd wait until the end of the day to record their thoughts and feelings. The resulting data? "Worthless!" Newman says.

By creating specialized apps for smartphones, psychologists have been able to monitor people's emotions and experiences several times a day and reap more nuanced reflections of their psychological state. In researching fluctuations in people with generalized anxiety disorder (GAD), Newman has used this minute documentation of their thoughts and feelings to challenge previous beliefs among some psychologists about the cause of the incessant worry that is the primary symptom of GAD. Earlier theories that were based on people's summaries of their feelings posited that individuals worry in order to mute negative feelings.

Newman's research suggests the opposite: incessant worry acts to sustain negative emotions. In one study, she and her colleagues monitored 83 people with GAD over eight days just before or right after a social interaction that lasted a minute or more. On average, the scientists found that people with GAD generally felt better after these social interactions, which suggests that the encounters were probably pleasant or at least benign. Counterintuitively, she found that those who worried less before the social encounter had more feelings such as anxiety and sadness after it. Those who worried more before the encounter felt happier or more contented afterward.

This study confirmed Newman's theory that anxious people believe that if they worry about a bad outcome (no matter how unlikely it is to occur), they won't experience the gut punch of something awful happening to them after they let themselves feel happy and optimistic. When a bad thing doesn't happen, she says, they feel relief, which reinforces their belief that worry protects them. Without these detailed logs of fluctuations in thoughts and feelings throughout the day, the study would have missed such insights.

Data gathered at frequent intervals also help therapists shape treatments adapted to individual patients. Many people don't know or may not remember what triggers their anxiety, but therapists can ferret it out by linking higher anxiety levels to in-the-moment events. They can prompt a patient to employ specific strategies learned previously in therapy to counter their worry. For example, using a technique called cognitive restructuring, patients might compare things that they worry might happen with real events to help them realize their worries are baseless.

Anxious people don't have only negative feelings, but they tend to minimize the positive ones. "We don't just want to lower negative feelings," Newman says. "We also need to enhance positive feelings."

To reinforce good feelings, Newman's colleague, Skidmore College psychologist Lucas LaFreniere, created a phone app called SkillJoy. Several times a day at random intervals, the app prompts anxious people to focus on an enjoyable thing in the present moment–such as seeing a friend, making someone laugh or hearing a great song–and to really "savor" what they are contemplating for a minute or two. A 2023 study found that after seven days, SkillJoy users worried less than they did before using the app.

This understanding of emotional flux throughout the course of the day has led researchers to ask whether a high level of IIV works for or against people. Newman's opinion in this debate is firm. "Variability is good," she says, "and there is no clear answer about when it indicates psychopathology." Others in the field are less certain. Whereas some studies have linked high variability with neuroticism, others have failed to do so. A lot depends on context. A person with high IIV, Ram says, may be successfully adapting to a tumultuous life, and someone with lower IIV may have a predictable, routinized life and may actually be more rigid.

According to studies by scholars such as University of Michigan social scientist Lizbeth Benson, having a greater variety of emotions that range from enthusiasm and determination to sadness and fear—dubbed emodiversity by Jordi Quoidbach, an associate professor at Esade Law School in Barcelona—is thought to help people better adjust to different situations over the course of the day. "The coolest thing we showed is that for those who experienced high levels of negative emotion," Benson says, those who had more kinds of negative emotions tended to have better health outcomes.

For therapists and patients, acknowledging the highs and lows of daily emotions—some bad, others eminently good; some moods way up, others beyond down—has provided new insights for the enduring goal of psychology to help define who we are so we can learn to live with that knowledge and find ways to more fully become the people we want to be.

About the Author

Francine Russo is a veteran journalist specializing in social sciences and relationships. She is author of Love after 50: How to Find It, Enjoy It, and Keep It *(Simon and Schuster, 2021).*

Control Your Feelings in 5 Stages

By Steve Ayan

Once upon a time people firmly believed that thinking and feeling were two separate capacities, destined to often clash. As 17th-century Dutch philosopher Baruch de Spinoza put it, "When a man is prey to his emotions, he is not his own master, but lies at the mercy of fortune." By this logic, the intensity of experiences such as sadness, anger or fear can trump our reasoning. Yet modern research tells us otherwise. We are not slaves to our passing passions; rather we regulate emotions all of the time. You resist exploding at a client just because he is tardy, and you manage not to throw things at the house next door during their noisy barbecue. Controlling anger and frustration keeps our professional and private lives on track–and prevents irksome situations from escalating.

Regulating emotions goes beyond keeping them down. We also need to find healthy outlets for our feelings. These inner responses, after all, can be excellent guides, as when fear warns you off a risky choice. They enrich daily life as well, leading us to revel in the joy of a birthday party or hoot ecstatically when a favorite team wins a game.

How exactly we go about striking a balance with our emotions is a topic that psychologists have been plumbing for decades. Their work has underscored that there is no single perfect approach. A good option in one case could be cataclysmic in another scenario. Instead we rely on dozens of techniques.

To make sense of these disparate tactics, psychologist James Gross of Stanford University developed a model in 1998 that sought to explain how emotions arise. Gross argued that any emotional experience follows a trajectory with five distinct stages in which a person can intervene to alter the outcome. At first we decide whether to seek out or avoid an emotional scenario. Then we may modify the situation itself. In the next two stages, we sideline unhelpful feelings by redirecting our attention or reappraising our response. Finally, we can deploy coping mechanisms to handle the physiological and behavioral consequences of an emotional event. The comprehensive scope and simplicity of Gross's model quickly made it the most influential framework for emotion regulation in the field.

The catch, however, is that most of our responses at each stage are automatic. How we react in the face of calamity is often the result of habit or circumstance rather than deliberate choice. "The learned set of emotion regulation behaviors is powerful and not easy to modify," says University of California, Berkeley, psychologist Iris Mauss.

Yet we can learn complementary techniques to make the most of our knee-jerk responses. Current research has confirmed that with a little training and awareness, we can learn to avoid potential pitfalls and prevail over every part of this process. By heightening sensitivity to long-term goals, the broader context of an event and a feeling's intensity, we can make smart choices in even fraught situations. In short, we can master our emotions.

Stage 1: Pick and Choose

It is a rainy Friday afternoon. You have had an exhausting week, and you want nothing more than to curl up on the couch and take a nap. You had planned to spend a long, lonely evening working on your taxes. Then a friend calls to ask if you want to see a movie instead.

You are facing the very first stage in Gross's model: "situation selection." You have the power to choose the path your evening will take and the emotional outcome of your day. Here you have to engage in some psychological fortune-telling. How might an evening of taxes make you feel in the future? If you see the movie instead, how will your Saturday shape up? This task can be challenging. Spending time with a friend may be restorative–or it might lead you to neglect necessary chores.

Before you decide, bear in mind that people routinely overestimate the intensity of future emotions. Numerous studies have shown that negative outcomes are often not as bad as we expect, and sometimes pursuing a seemingly more positive option can inadvertently set us up for disappointment. For example, in findings published in 2011 Mauss and several colleagues asked 69 participants to read either an article extolling the value of happiness or an emotionally neutral story. Afterward the participants watched a feel-good film clip. Curiously, the people who had read about the benefits of happiness felt less cheery after the movie than the participants who had not read the article. Why the paradox? Mauss theorizes that a preoccupation with being happy can lead people to expect too much from everyday pleasures. Additionally, evaluating your level of bliss may heighten self-awareness, which could hinder the experience of pleasure when it comes your way.

Psychologist Maya Tamir of the Hebrew University of Jerusalem has found that rather than making the pursuit of happiness a guiding principle in life, a person should think in terms of broader aims. In 2012 Tamir and Brett Q. Ford, now at the University of Toronto, gave 136 people a battery of tests, including one designed to assess emotional intelligence, which is the ability to recognize, control and express emotions. The participants pondered situations and selected the emotion they would prefer to experience in that moment. For example, "If you need to reach a compromise, would you rather feel angry or happy?"

Tamir and Ford found that people with high emotional intelligence opted for whichever feeling had greatest utility–regardless of whether that emotion was pleasant. A little anger might help an otherwise easygoing person prepare for a difficult negotiation, and piquing anxiety could create extra incentive to study for an exam. A good policy, then, is to keep your long-term goals in mind when evaluating a decision such as how to spend your Friday evening.

Stage 2: Take Action

Often people face an emotional event with no way to change course. Perhaps they have to read a eulogy at a funeral or sit next to a particularly irksome aunt during a holiday meal. In these cases, the best options involve "situation modification," or changing elements of the environment to make things easier.

The key is to anticipate the potential for stress and take proactive measures. These interventions can be as simple as carrying a lucky charm to make you feel more comfortable or asking a friend to sit nearby as a conversational buffer. Such strategies can also avert further annoyance. For example, if a neighbor is making a lot of noise, you may be better served asking him to quiet down now rather than waiting it out and becoming more frustrated.

Recent research suggests that people who do not take steps to ease difficult circumstances will only compound their troubles. In 2013 Franklin & Marshall College psychologist Allison S. Troy, along with Mauss and New York University mindfulness researcher Amanda Shallcross, recruited 170 volunteers who had experienced a challenging life event in the two months prior to the study. The experimenters first rated how controllable these events were–ranging from accidents and illnesses that no one could have foreseen to things caused directly by the individual's actions, such as losing a job because of poor performance. Next, the volunteers watched a sad movie while consciously trying to view the film in a positive light.

Some people found this task to be more taxing than others did. Among the participants who were very successful in reframing the film, those whose recent history had included a stressful but controllable event, such as getting fired because of shoddy work, reported more symptoms of depression than counterparts whose experiences had been less controllable. Events that could have been averted left people more susceptible to depression, perhaps because their failure to prevent problems primed them for feelings of hopelessness. And people who could recast a negative event in a positive way may be most at risk because their flexible thinking allows them to recognize different outcomes to their earlier life events. Individuals in controllable scenarios, therefore, should identify and address sources of stress proactively rather than assuming they can manage the emotional fallout later.

Stage 3: Look Elsewhere

When it is too late to change any aspect of a situation, Gross proposed that people deploy their attention to their advantage, either through distraction or through focus on the matter at hand. For instance, if you need to keep a serious demeanor during an important professional meeting, you might avoid glancing at a colleague who enjoys clowning around during work hours.

Whether you should concentrate your attention or divert it will depend in part on the situation's intensity. In a series of studies, psychologist Gal Sheppes of Tel Aviv University asked participants to either reinterpret a sad photograph in a way that made it less worrisome–seeing tears of joy as opposed to grief, for example–or think of something completely different. Although people who reimagined an image's meaning could alter their emotional response, participants often opted for avoidance. Sheppes found that the more unsettling an image was, the more often people preferred to self-distract. This result suggests that attending to a powerful stimulus can be exhausting, making the opportunity to look away a welcome relief.

In 2014 Sheppes took these findings a step further. He asked 22 participants to look at photographs with varying emotional intensities. This time, however, he gave them additional information. He instructed some of the subjects to respond in a way that would minimize their immediate negative feelings and told other participants that they would have to confront this image later in the experiment. Once again, most people looked away when an image was especially distressing, but those who believed they would view the image in the future were more likely to study even the intense pictures. Distraction, therefore, is an easy option but not necessarily the best way to respond to a recurring concern.

Admittedly, controlling attention can be a challenge: our thoughts and gaze often wander despite our best efforts. Yet certain therapies might help. For example, working memory training, which bolsters the brain's ability to hold and manipulate multiple pieces of information, can boost many facets of emotion regulation, including attention. Typically this training involves learning memory strategies, such as mental rehearsal and mnemonic devices, and doing exercises that use working memory. In addition, mindfulness-based stress-reduction therapy can teach practitioners to observe and detach from inner reactions to strengthen emotional management. In 2010 Gross and Philippe Goldin, now at the University of California, Davis, found that eight sessions of this therapy and a half-day meditation retreat could help people with social anxiety disorder learn to attend to their breathing to refocus during an unpleasant experience.

Stage 4: Think Again

The people in Sheppes's 2014 study who did not look away from disturbing photographs engaged in a process that psychologists call "cognitive change" or reappraisal. This is when individuals tackle thoughts that lead to an emotional response. For example, a performer with stage fright might reframe nervous energy as "getting pumped" for his next show.

In its most extreme form, some people engage in this stage through prolonged pondering of their personal experiences and sensations. This practice, known as rumination, can intensify symptoms of depression and aggression. A better technique, according to psychologists Ethan Kross of the University of Michigan and Ozlem Ayduk of U.C. Berkeley, is "self-distancing," or imagining the situation as an impartial observer. Instead of asking "Why do I feel like that?" they recommend addressing the question in the third person: "Why does Steve feel like that?"

In 2012 Kross, working with colleagues at Ohio State University and VU University in the Netherlands, published findings from a study in which they examined how self-distancing strategies affect feelings and behaviors. In the first experiment they asked

94 volunteers to rapidly solve anagram puzzles and then announce their solutions aloud. The experimenters, meanwhile, stoked the students' ire by repeatedly demanding that the speaker raise his or her voice. After this activity the students had to visualize the events that had just taken place in one of three ways: as they themselves experienced them, as though they had been a mere witness to the events, or without any special instructions.

Kross and his colleagues found that the participants who imagined the events as though they had been bystanders harbored significantly fewer aggressive thoughts and feelings than their colleagues who had relived the preceding moments. In a follow-up experiment, students who used this fly-on-the-wall perspective for thinking about an emotional moment showed less aggressive behavior than their peers who had not employed self-distancing.

Stage 5: Let It Out

But what if, despite your best efforts, you still find yourself walloped by an emotional blow? If someone unexpectedly shares an insulting opinion, for example, you might not be able to avoid feeling hurt, but you can still respond in many ways. Your jaw might drop in indignation, you could take a deep breath to calm your rising pulse, or you might smile and act unfazed. In the final stage of regulation your options are limited to managing your bodily response.

A person's immediate reaction may be dictated by personality, experience or culture. For example, many Western societies advocate venting, or the release of stress through conversation or exercise. Unfortunately, these techniques can sometimes fuel a person's fury further, revving up energy instead of releasing it.

The primary strategy that people employ at this stage is suppressing their physical reactions. This response results in part from parents raising their children to behave in this way. Not screaming, hitting or crying whenever you feel like it is an integral part of socialization—but holding back emotions can take a toll. In a classic experiment, psychologist Roy F. Baumeister of Florida

State University found that when people restrained their emotions during either a comical or sad film clip they tended to give up earlier on a subsequent anagram puzzle than participants who could express their feelings. Resisting emotional responses had taxed their willpower and energy.

This stress and exhaustion could explain why inhibited expression of feelings is linked to health problems. Johan Denollet and his colleagues at Tilburg University in the Netherlands found in 2010 that people who regularly suppress their emotional distress–a pattern called type D personality–have an increased risk of cardiovascular disease. Denollet has also found that those who hold back emotions suffer more from chronic pain, tinnitus and diabetes than the general population.

Suppression can also put your relationships at risk, as psychologist Emily Impett of the University of Toronto and her colleagues discovered in a 2012 study. In a survey of 80 couples, Impett learned that men and women felt emotionally distanced when they discovered that their significant other had not disclosed his or her feelings in the past. In a follow-up three months later the researchers found that "suppressor couples" had worse-functioning partnerships than other participants.

In addition, a host of studies make it evident that positive feelings are far easier to squash than negative ones. Restraining your response–whether smiling in spite of your sadness or holding back an inappropriate giggle–is ultimately a powerful strategy that should be used sparingly.

The lessons from suppression research are an important reminder that regulating emotions need not mean avoiding them. Instead people can learn to better anticipate their own reactions to intense moments, visualize the outcomes they would prefer and identify the actions that could change those future feelings. By acknowledging and exploring why we feel a certain way, we can use both happy and troubling events to our advantage. They may even prompt us to dig into our beliefs, experiences and misconceptions–and discover new insights into ourselves.

Five Tips for Emotional Health

Emotions are hard to control. But even without a fully fledged strategy for regulation, you can adopt some basic techniques to improve your well-being:

1. Be active. Physical exercise and intellectual engagement usually prevent people from focusing on negative emotions too much. Strain your body once in a while at the gym or enjoy good food, books and music. Such pastimes can make it easier to look at the bright side of life.
2. Try new habits. Disrupting your routine can help you focus on positive events and avoid boredom. For example, start a diary and take note of nice things that happen to you. Reserve a few minutes each day to remind yourself of happy times.
3. Be social. Mingle with folks you like. An active social life is an effective means to overcome everyday worries and mild anxieties.
4. Be thankful. Being grateful for what you have received enhances satisfaction.
5. Don't set the bar too high. It is possible to want happiness too much. Putting pressure on yourself to be merry all of the time may itself become a source of discontent. It is okay–and healthy–to experience a whole spectrum of emotions.

About the Author

Steve Ayan is a psychologist and an editor at Gehirn&Geist.

Sleep Deprivation Sometimes Relieves Depression. A New Study May Show Why

By Emily Willingham

In 1818 Johann Christian August Heinroth, considered to have been the first professor of psychiatry at a university, suggested that sleep deprivation might alleviate "melancholia," or depression. But it wasn't until 1959 that formal reports began to emerge, again from Germany, suggesting that a night of sleeplessness could boost mood in depression. Experimental trials in the 1970s went on to confirm a benefit. Since then study after study has shown that spending a night without sleep, especially with lights on, indeed produces mood benefits for about half of the people with depression.

The effects of this approach, dubbed "wake therapy," offer the bonus of being immediate, unlike most antidepressants, which require a few weeks to work. Sleep deprivation has disadvantages that include, well, going without sleep. As anyone who has parented an infant can attest, that has unwanted "spillover" effects on other aspects of life. Identifying processes in the brain that underlie sleep-deprived boosting of mood could lead to therapies that are less burdensome than enduring a wakeful night.

A new study published June 20 in the *Proceedings of the National Academy of Sciences USA* has identified specific brain regions that kick up activity when sleep deprivation lifts one's mood. Because the research included people with and without depression, the findings broaden understanding about the "bizarre phenomenon" of mood-boosting sleep deprivation, says study author Philip Gehrman, a professor of clinical psychology at the University of Pennsylvania.

Even without immediately leading to new therapies, the results confirm the benefit of wake therapy in depression, says Anna Wirz-Justice, a professor emerita at the Center for Chronobiology at the University Psychiatric Clinics Basel in Switzerland, who was not involved in the work. "Perhaps this study, which provides clues to mechanisms, will lead to reevaluation of the intervention as an inexpensive, rapid antidepressant modality."

To take a peek inside the brain, Gehrman and his colleagues evaluated 30 people with major depressive disorder who all underwent sleep deprivation. They also assessed another 54 people without depression, 16 of whom served as controls who did not undergo sleep deprivation.

Over the course of five days, researchers performed three imaging scans on all of the participants. The sleep deprivation groups underwent one scan after a normal night's sleep, another after a sleepless night and a third after two nights of recovery sleep. The 16 control participants without depression underwent three scans, too, but got regular sleep. The scanning tracked blood oxygen delivery in the brains of participants as they lay still, doing nothing. In between scans, every two waking hours from days two to five, all participants completed a questionnaire assessing their mood.

The questionnaire responses showed that 43 percent of those with diagnosed depression experienced mood improvement after sleep deprivation. Most, but not all, of those without depression reported a worsened mood after losing sleep.

Imaging in those reporting improved mood showed increased activity in two brain regions that were previously implicated in depression and the effects of sleep deprivation. One of these regions, the amygdala, is famously associated with emotion processing and memory. The other is the anterior cingulate cortex, which studies have connected to depression and to the benefits of sleep deprivation. Unexpectedly, activity in these two areas was increased in participants whose mood improved whether they had depression or not.

The involvement of the anterior cingulate cortex "fits the picture" that these previous studies have pieced together about depression and disrupted sleep, says Francesco Benedetti, a longtime sleep disruption researcher at the department of clinical neurosciences at San Raffaele Hospital in Milan, who was not involved in the work.

The implied link between the two regions suggests that they have a role in producing an elevated mood after a sleepless night. In participants with depression, the connection persisted even after two nights of recovery sleep. Benedetti says that sleep deprivation may heighten the effect of structures in the upper part of the brain, such as the anterior cingulate cortex, on quieting the amygdala and boosting mood. This signal in people reporting mood improvement regardless of depression diagnosis is "an important clue" to understanding how sleep deprivation works, Wirz-Justice says. Studies like this are a "fabulous" way to study what underlies changes in mood without interference from medications, she adds.

Back in 1976 Burkhard Pflug, a psychiatrist at the University of Tubingen in Germany, wrote that sleep deprivation might behave like a "zeitgeber," or "time giver," in people with depression and resynchronize aberrant brain rhythms. Benedetti's work indicates that depression might flatten rhythmic cycles that support brain function and that sleep deprivation might jump-start these rhythms back into a healthy pattern.

The new findings may offer targets for reviving the zeitgeber in depression in accessible ways. A noninvasive technique called transcranial magnetic stimulation, in which magnetic waves are applied from outside the skull, is used to treat depression, but its effectiveness relies on hitting the right regions. Gehrman says that brain circuits that are responsive to sleep deprivation could represent candidate targets for transcranial magnetic stimulation or other kinds of stimulation. Such approaches hold potential to produce the rapid effect of sleep deprivation without the downside of a sleepless night.

About the Author

Emily Willingham is a science writer and author of the books Phallacy: Life Lessons from the Animal Penis *(Avery, Penguin Publishing Group, 2020) and* The Tailored Brain: From Ketamine, to Keto, to Companionship: A User's Guide to Feeling Better and Thinking Smarter *(Basic Books, 2021).*

Why Sleep Deprivation Makes You Crabby

By Tori Rodriguez

When you're tired, it can seem as if everything is filtered through a negative lens. That might be because your positive lens is fuzzy when you are sleep-deprived, according to findings of two related studies published last year in the *Journal of Psychosomatic Research*. Two groups of college students completed a series of tests to assess their emotional responses to negative and positive pictures, similar to those often shown on the nightly news. Twenty-eight students completed the test at various points throughout a night of simulated shift work after getting five hours of sleep, and 31 students did the same after staying awake for more than 24 hours. The students completed a short survey to indicate how each picture made them feel.

The researchers found that all subjects' emotional response to the photographs became increasingly dampened as the night wore on, and their reaction to positive stimuli was even more subdued—that is, they grew less likely to feel good in response to uplifting pictures. "The human brain is naturally more attentive to negative events," perhaps as a survival mechanism that keeps us on the alert for life-threatening situations, says study co-author June J. Pilcher, a psychologist at Clemson University. Yet in modern society, life-threatening events are fairly rare, so instead we find ourselves overreacting to the pile of dirty dishes—especially when we, ourselves, are washed-out.

About the Author

Tori Rodriguez is a journalist and psychotherapist based in Atlanta. Her writing has also appeared in the Atlantic, Women's Health *and* Real Simple.

Why Sleep-Deprived People Are More Selfish and Lonely

By Daisy Yuhas

How did you sleep last night? For many people, the answer is "not great." In the U.S., about a third of people get fewer than seven hours of shut-eye, which is the minimum recommendation. Most of us are familiar with the unpleasant results. We may feel groggy and grumpy, and everything gets just a bit harder to do. But sleeplessness also impairs parts of the brain that affect our social lives and abilities to relate to other people, according to research by neuroscientist Eti Ben Simon, a postdoctoral fellow at the University of California, Berkeley. People who sleep less are less likely to help others, for instance. Ben Simon spoke with Mind Matters editor Daisy Yuhas to discuss what the social consequences of bad sleep are and how good sleep can be leveraged to benefit well-being.

[An edited transcript of the interview follows.]

Q: In past research, you and your colleagues have found that lack of sleep contributes to anxiety and difficulty managing emotions. In addition, you've recently found that poor sleep affects social interactions, regardless of mood. How does that work?

A: People are less interested in social interaction when they're sleep-deprived. For example, we designed a task where an experimenter and participant would face each other, and they would walk toward each other. The participant would decide when someone got too close, and we would measure that distance. Consistently, when people were sleep-deprived, they preferred others to be farther away.

Mood may play a part in the social consequences of sleep loss, but it's not the whole story. We've controlled for mood in studies of social behavior and seen that social withdrawal is not just an effect of mood.

We've also found that sleep deprivation reduces activity in what's known as the theory of mind network in the brain. These are areas that help us think about other people—what they might want, what they're like, and how they are similar to or different from ourselves.

Q: How might those changes in the brain relate to our thinking?

A: In a recent study, we explored that by asking participants—either after they had a full night's sleep or after they had had no sleep—to think about different individuals while their brain activity was being recorded in an fMRI [functional magnetic resonance imaging] scanner. Then they answered a questionnaire that explored how likely they were to help others. We asked about daily acts, such as keeping the elevator door open, helping someone with their grocery bags, things like that.

We found that sleep-deprived people were significantly less likely to want to help others, and that correlated one to one with the impairment in their theory of mind network. The larger the impairment, the less they wanted to help other people. And it didn't matter if it was helping a friend, a family member or a stranger.

Q: Total sleep deprivation is pretty extreme. What if people get at least some sleep?

A: In a second study, we used the same questionnaire, but this time, we tracked people's natural sleep across four nights and days. We didn't find any association with how much people slept in hours, but we found that the *quality* of their sleep—how many times they woke up during the night, whether they had a restful sleep or their sleep was fragmented—determined whether they were likely to want to help others or not.

Q: So people who sleep poorly say they don't want to help others. But have you found that sleep deprivation changes actual helping behaviors in a noticeable way?

A: Yes. In a third study, we looked at a database of charitable donations and compared the week of [the transition to] daylight saving time–when people lose, on average, an hour of sleep–to other weeks of the year. In 15 years' worth of data, we kept seeing that on that week, the amount people donate is reduced by about 10 percent.

In Arizona and Hawaii, states that don't do daylight saving, we don't see this effect. We also looked at the switch to standard time, when people "fall back," and didn't find an effect either. Putting these data together, we could demonstrate that lack of sleep may be impairing altruistic sentiment across the U.S.

Other researchers are looking at similar questions. Just a few months ago a colleague of mine published a study that found doctors prescribe fewer painkillers during a night shift than a day shift, and that was accompanied by reduced empathy for their patients.

Q: You've also found that one person's sleeplessness affects everyone around them. How does that happen?

A: In general, our ability to pick up that something's off with the person we're interacting with is really magnificent. In one study, just a one-minute video clip of someone talking was enough for others to pick up that they didn't want to interact with a sleep-deprived person.

Sleep deprivation can make people feel lonely, and we've found that when people come into contact with someone who is sleep deprived, they report feeling lonelier after that interaction. I like to say that helps settle the Beatles' question: "All the lonely people, where do they all come from?" It all started with sleep loss.

More seriously, I worry about a negative feedback loop with loneliness. If you're chronically sleep-deprived, that feeling of not connecting can just keep increasing. You're more withdrawn, less interested in interacting with others, and we've shown that others are less interested in interacting with you.

Q: Could that in turn contribute to the connection between sleep and conditions such as anxiety or depression?

A: There is an intimate link between mental health and lack of sleep. We know that people suffering from disrupted sleep are also more likely to develop anxiety and depression down the line. With anxiety, for instance, when something stresses you out, the first thing that gets impaired is your sleep. And paradoxically, more sleep is what you need to feel calmer.

Q: We're such social beings. Why would our sleepy brain shut down the network that helps us connect with others?

A: The brain and body need sleep so much that they start letting go of whatever we don't immediately need once sleep is missing. In nature, the only time you see animals sleep-deprived is when they're migrating, they just had a baby or they're starving. So being sleep-deprived is really a stress signal that makes us want to accumulate as much food as we can and be more alert to threats. We don't have the capacity for anything more than that.

The more time you spend awake, the more sleep becomes the one thing that you need to focus on. Everything else just goes in the background.

Q: On the flip side, does this mean we should really put better sleep alongside diet and exercise as a crucial way to improve mental health?

A: Exactly. Sleep is something that can help us intervene into social and emotional affective disorders; it's another way into mental health.

Sleep is actually the bedrock, even before diet and exercise. The way we metabolize food and the way our muscles react also depends on good sleep.

It's not always easy to restore good sleep. But once we prioritize it, we can really help shift symptoms, mood, anxiety and even the desire to be kind to other people.

About the Author

Daisy Yuhas edits the Scientific American *column Mind Matters. She is a freelance science journalist and editor based in Austin, Tex. She is author of the* Kids Field Guide to Birds.

Why Just One Sleepless Night Makes People Emotionally Fragile

By Eti Ben Simon

When I was a graduate student, my colleagues and I studied how losing one night of sleep affects a person's ability to manage their emotions. Once a week, typically on a Friday evening, I would stay up all night to monitor our participants and ensure that they followed the protocol. At about noon the next day, we would all stumble out of the laboratory, exhausted and eager to get home and rest.

Two months into the experiment, I was in my car at a traffic light when a silly love song started playing on the radio. Suddenly, I was crying uncontrollably. I remember feeling surprised at my reaction. It then hit me that I was not just studying sleep deprivation—I had become *part* of the study. Weeks of missed sleep had taken their toll, and I was no longer in control of my emotions.

That research project, and many that have followed since, demonstrated a strong and intimate link between better sleep and emotional health. In healthy individuals, good-quality sleep is linked with a more positive mood—and it takes just one night of sleep deprivation to trigger a robust spike in anxiety and depression the following morning. Moreover, people who suffer from chronic sleep disruption tend to experience daily events as more negative, making it hard to escape a gloomy mindset. Indeed, in a national sleep survey, 85 percent of Americans reported mood disruption when they were not able to get enough sleep.

Studies from our lab and others are now beginning to illuminate just how a lack of sleep frays the inner fabric of our mind. One of its many impacts is to disrupt the brain's circuitry for regulating emotions.

For decades researchers and medical professionals considered sleep loss a by-product or symptom of another, more "primary" condition, such as depression or anxiety. In other words, *first* comes the anxiety, and then sleep loss follows. Today we know that this order can be reversed. In fact, sleep loss and anxiety, depression or other mental health conditions may feed into one another, creating a downward spiral that is exceedingly difficult to break.

Much evidence in this area comes from chronic sleeplessness or insomnia. People who suffer from insomnia are at least twice as likely to develop depression or anxiety later in life, compared with individuals who sleep well. For instance, a study that followed 1,500 individuals–some with insomnia and others without–found that chronic sleeplessness was associated with a three times greater increase in the onset of depression a year later and twice the increase in the onset of anxiety.

Insomnia symptoms also raise the risk of developing post-traumatic stress disorder and track closely with suicidal behavior among at-risk individuals. They often precede a mood episode in people with bipolar disorder. Even after adequate treatment for depression or anxiety, people who continue to suffer from sleep difficulties are at greater risk of relapse relative to those whose sleep improves. Understanding sleep's role in this pattern could unlock insights for helping to prevent and treat many emotional and mental disorders.

Older research already revealed that sleep loss can precede serious mental health symptoms in otherwise healthy individuals. In studies conducted mostly in the 1960s, volunteers who stayed awake for more than two nights reported difficulties forming thoughts, finding words and composing sentences. They suffered from hallucinations, such as seeing inanimate objects move or experiencing the sensation of another's touch despite being alone. After three days without sleep, some participants became delusional and paranoid. They believed they were secret agents or that aliens were contacting them. (If that sounds like a psychotic episode, that's because it is.) After five days, several participants entered a state resembling a full-blown clinical psychosis and were unable to fully comprehend their circumstances.

In one study from 1947, volunteers from the U.S. military attempted to stay awake for more than four nights. A soldier who was described by his friends as quiet and reserved became extremely aggressive after three nights without sleep. He provoked fights and insisted he was on a secret mission for the president. Eventually he was forcibly restrained and dismissed from the experiment. Six others exhibited outbursts of violence and persistent hallucinations. In all cases, after sleeping for an entire day, the soldiers behaved normally again and had no recollection of the earlier mayhem. In another study, in which participants stayed awake for four nights, researchers were unprepared for the "frequent psychotic features" they encountered, such as intense hallucinations and paranoid delusions.

Given these destructive effects, studies of prolonged sleep loss are now considered to be unethical, but they still offer a powerful reminder of just how sleep-dependent our minds and mental health truly are.

Even with these startling results, scientists have been skeptical about the consequences of restless nights, particularly given that (fortunately) few of us endure such extreme deprivation. That's where the newest wave of research comes in. In recent years a neuroscientific explanation has emerged that is beginning to illuminate what it is about sleep, or the lack of it, that seems to have a direct link to our emotions.

Whenever we face a nerve-wracking or emotionally intense challenge, a hub deep in the brain called the amygdala kicks into gear. The amygdala can trigger a comprehensive whole-body response to prepare us for the challenge or threat we face. This flight-or-fight response increases our heart rate and sends a wave of stress hormones rushing into our bloodstream. Luckily, there's one brain region standing between us and this cascade of hyperarousal: the prefrontal cortex, an area right behind the middle of our eyebrows. Studies show that activity in this region tends to dampen, or downregulate, the amygdala, thus keeping our emotional response under control.

In studies where my colleagues and I deprived healthy volunteers of one night of sleep, they discovered that the activity of the prefrontal cortex dropped drastically, as measured using functional magnetic resonance imaging (fMRI). Moreover, the neural activity linking the amygdala and the prefrontal cortex became significantly weaker. In other words, both the region and the circuit meant to keep our emotional reactions under control are essentially out of order when sleep is disrupted. Other studies have found that this profile of neural impairment can occur in people after they experience just one night of sleep deprivation, in people who are habitual short sleepers, or when participants' sleep is restricted to only four hours a night for five nights.

This impairment can be so robust that it blurs the lines around what people consider emotional. For example, when my colleagues and I exposed participants to neutral and emotional pictures (think bland images of commuters on a train versus photographs of children crying), fMRI revealed that the amygdala responded differently to these prompts when people were well rested. But after losing a night of sleep, a person's amygdala responded strongly to *both* kinds of images. In other words, the threshold for what the brain deems emotional became significantly lower when the amygdala could not act in concert with the prefrontal cortex. Such impaired emotional control makes us more vulnerable to anxiety and poor mood, so that even silly love songs can trigger sobbing.

The effects on the amygdala, the prefrontal cortex and the circuitry between the two may have many other consequences as well. In January we published findings that show that changes in this brain circuit, together with other regions involved in arousal, relate to increases in blood pressure after one night of sleep loss. The brain-level mechanisms my colleagues and I have observed may contribute to changes that negatively affect the entire body, increasing the risk for hypertension and cardiovascular disease.

Stepping back, it becomes clear that–like our physical well-being–mental and emotional health rely on a delicate balance. Myriad choices we make throughout the day *and* night maintain that balance. Even a single sleepless night can therefore do damage. We need to be mindful of this reality, for both ourselves and one another. Inevitably we all miss out on sleep from time to time. But our societies should critically examine structures–such as work norms, school cultures, and the lack of support for parents or other caregivers–that prevent people from getting enough rest. The science of sleep and mental health suggests that failing to address those problems will leave people vulnerable to serious harm.

About the Author

Eti Ben Simon is a research scientist at the University of California, Berkeley. She studies the emotional and social consequences of sleep loss on the human brain and body.

How Humor Takes the Edge off Hard Times

By Meghan Bartels

Three psychologists walk into a bar to compose a witty toast to the power of humor. Or rather I picked up the phone and called each of them about the subject. (I'm just terrible at telling jokes.) But these psychologists do genuinely want people to understand the role that humor can play in helping one deal with stress, anger, fear, anxiety and other difficult emotions. Sometimes, that means purposefully embracing humor when things are going well, shoring up defenses against hard times to come. And sometimes it can mean spontaneously laughing when you want to cry or cracking an absurdist joke when it feels like the sky is falling and Earth is on fire.

"There is this autopilot, unconscious way that many people engage humor without thinking about it," says Steven Sultanoff, a clinical psychologist and an adjunct professor at Pepperdine University. "It is a strategic coping mechanism, but it's not a conscious one."

To psychologists, a coping mechanism is any kind of behavior or thought someone uses to deal with stress, says Janet Gibson, a psychologist and a professor emerita at Grinnell College. Not all of these strategies are beneficial, she notes: drinking or binge eating, for example, are more dangerous coping mechanisms.

But humor is indeed a powerful way of handling stressors, which "activate how we feel, how we think, how we act–and our physiology," Sultanoff says. Humor does exactly the same things, just in a different direction.

Stress may make someone feel anxious or angry; humor replaces that feeling with a moment of joy, lightness, surprise or connection. In many situations, "when you're experiencing humor, you cannot experience distressing emotions," Sultanoff says. "These emotions dissolve." Stress may also narrow someone's thinking about a situation, whereas humor taps into creativity that can enable a perspective shift.

And of course, there's the physical embodiment of humor: laughter. With it comes better breathing, muscle relaxation and a higher pain tolerance, potentially caused by the release of endorphins. "The stress is there; you just don't feel it as much," Gibson says.

Humor is, moreover, inherently social. "We crave connection, especially when we are feeling heightened levels of stress," says Michele Tugade, a psychologist at Vassar College.

Of course, humor isn't foolproof: making the wrong joke the wrong way is just as likely to increase stress and disconnection. "Mean-spirited or disparaging humor actually causes people to be further apart and increases division," Tugade says.

Humor can arise during stress without a person making any effort to evoke it—or even necessarily understanding where it is coming from or why. But humor can also be cultivated, Sultanoff says, adding that he himself uses it as a conscious way of lightening the mood and building connections with people around him. He says that that he travels with a clown nose to facilitate finding fun in life's mundane moments. "Joyful use of humor builds psychological antibodies," he says.

Notwithstanding the occasional clown nose, embracing the power of humor doesn't mean subscribing to toxic positivity. The point is not to never feel difficult emotions, Tugade says. "Stress is there for a reason, and it's to call your attention to a problem that needs to be solved," she says. "When you experience a negative emotion like sadness or anger or frustration, it's important to recognize why that's there." Turning to humor too soon may prevent someone from processing emotions in a healthy way, increasing stress rather than decreasing it, she adds.

Instead consider expressing humor in moderation and as a moment of relief amid a seemingly constant onslaught of grim headlines and hard feelings. "You're not denying that there is some trouble in the world and there's great despair and grief," Tugade says. "It's giving yourself a break. And we all need a little break."

About the Author

Meghan Bartels is a science journalist based in New York City. She joined Scientific American *in 2023 and is now a senior news reporter there. Previously, she spent more than four years as a writer and editor at Space.com, as well as nearly a year as a science reporter at* Newsweek, *where she focused on space and Earth science. Her writing has also appeared in* Audubon, Nautilus, Astronomy *and* Smithsonian, *among other publications. She attended Georgetown University and earned a master's degree in journalism at New York University's Science, Health and Environmental Reporting Program.*

Forcing a Smile Using Electrical Stimulation Can Boost Your Mood

By Rachel Nuwer

The expression "a smile a day keeps the blues away" may have some credence beyond the realm of greeting card messages. The lingering question of whether a smile or frown lifts or depresses emotion has persisted for decades and is still actively debated.

In a new study, researchers sought a more definitive answer by using electrical muscle stimulation to literally force people to curl the corners of their mouth up or down into a smile or a frown. They found evidence that the physical act of making those expressions seems to directly impact human emotions, cause the person to feel more positive or negative.

The idea that the body plays a role in shaping how people feel and perceive the world is "old and fascinating," says Sebastian Korb, a senior lecturer in psychology at the University of Essex in England and senior author of the research, which was published in *Emotion*. "But it's not universally accepted." Korb says that the new study suggests that facial activity does seem to influence emotions and adds evidence to this long-standing but contentious hypothesis.

The role that facial expressions play in influencing human emotion has roots in the 19th century, when Charles Darwin and philosopher and psychologist William James both postulated that physiological changes in the body could have an effect on emotion. In the 20th century researchers began to focus on the effect of facial expression, and in the 1970s this idea was formally described as the "facial feedback hypothesis."

In the decades since then, the hypothesis has received mixed empirical support. In 1988 researchers in Germany published a study that has come to be known as the pen task. They divided participants into two groups and asked them to manipulate a pen with their mouth in different ways. Both groups held the pen straight out, perpendicular to their lips, but one group held the pen between their teeth, which facilitated a smilelike expression, while the other held the pen between their lips with their mouth closed, forming a kisslike expression. The participants then ranked how humorous they found a series of cartoons. Those whose mouth was stretched into a smile found the cartoons to be funnier than those with the expression that resembled a kiss, which the researchers interpreted as evidence supporting the facial feedback hypothesis.

The well-known study was challenged, however, in 2016, when a team of researchers–including Korb–tried to replicate the findings across 17 labs, each of which conducted a study with more than 100 participants. In contrast to the original study, the researchers' results did not reveal any significant evidence that supported the facial feedback hypothesis.

"Some people said we should forget about the hypothesis entirely," Korb says, "while others, like me, said, 'Wait a second–maybe we shouldn't throw the baby out with the bathwater.' I started thinking about how we could find other methods to manipulate muscles in a more controlled way than sticking a pen into your mouth."

For the new study, Korb and his colleagues turned to electrical stimulation–a method that allowed them to target specific muscles in the face for a specific amount of time. They placed electrodes on 58 participants' skin and gradually increased the current until it induced a contraction that forced the face into a frown or a smile. Anatomical variability among the participants meant that each one received a slightly different level of current to activate the targeted muscle.

Each participant was exposed multiple times for five seconds to several experimental conditions: smiling or frowning while looking at a blank screen; smiling while looking at a happy image, such as a beautiful beach; and frowning while looking at a depressing image, such as a beach covered in garbage. They also performed the same set of experiments with weaker stimulations that did not produce any visible movement of participants' facial muscles. After being exposed to each condition, the participants ranked how positive or negative they felt.

Across all measures, the researchers found correlations between the participants' facial features and how they said they were feeling but no change in mood when they were exposed to the weaker stimulation. The strongest correlation occurred when smiles were paired with positive images. In the absence of the accompanying imagery, though, participants still ranked their mood lower when their facial muscles were forced to frown and higher when they were stimulated to smile. For the image-free findings, "the effect was not massive," Korb says. "But remember, we're only activating certain muscles to a very small degree for five seconds, so we're already putting ourselves in a situation where it's not obvious that we'd find an effect."

Heather Lench, a professor of psychological and brain sciences at Texas A&M University, who was not involved in the research, says the new study was done well and "opens up a new way to induce facial expressions."

Now that Korb and his colleagues have preliminary confirmation that the method works, they are planning additional studies, he says. Future research could investigate how activating different muscles in the face makes people feel or use electroencephalograms to determine how quickly the brain emotionally responds to those changes. Further work will also be needed, he adds, to untangle the more difficult question of whether it is truly the activity of facial muscles that influences emotion–or whether study participants are simply realizing that these muscles are being activated, which makes them think about the corresponding emotion.

Lench adds that there could also be practical applications for Korb and his colleagues' findings. "If there is a decently strong relationship between muscle activation and emotion, it opens up an interesting application of the work–that people could self-stimulate their muscles using wearable devices, for example, to change their emotional state," she says. "The health, ethical and societal implications of this kind of application are very interesting."

About the Author

Rachel Nuwer is a science journalist and author. Her latest book is I Feel Love: MDMA and the Quest for Connection in a Fractured World *(Bloomsbury, 2023). Follow her on X: @RachelNuwer*

GLOSSARY

aberrant Straying from the right or normal way.

acquiescent Tending to accept or allow what others want or demand.

astute Mentally sharp or clever.

bereavement The state or fact of being deprived of something or someone.

bigotry Obstinate or intolerant devotion to one's own opinions and prejudices.

blasé Apathetic to pleasure or excitement as a result of excessive indulgence or enjoyment.

calibrated Standardized by determining the deviation from a standard (of something, such as a measuring instrument) so as to ascertain the proper correction factors.

canvassers People who go through (a district) or go to (other persons) in order to solicit orders or political support or to determine opinions or sentiments.

catalyze To alter significantly.

collectivist A political or economic theory advocating collective control especially over production and distribution.

conciliatory Intended to gain goodwill or favor or to reduce hostility.

contentious Likely to cause disagreement or argument.

electroconvulsive Of, relating to, or involving convulsive response to electroshock.

electroencephalograms The tracing of brain waves made by an electroencephalograph.

eudaemonic Producing happiness: based on the idea of happiness as the proper end of conduct.

hedonic Of, relating to, or characterized by pleasure.

ire Intense and usually openly displayed anger.

neuromodulation A treatment that alters nerve activity to treat neurological disorders.

nuanced Having or characterized by subtle and often appealingly complex qualities, aspects, or distinctions (as in character or tone).

olfaction The act or process of smelling.

palpable Capable of being touched or felt.

pernicious Highly injurious or destructive.

pheromones Chemical substances that are usually produced by an animal and serve especially as stimuli to other individuals of the same species for one or more behavioral responses.

precipice At the point of onset of a hazardous situation.

preponderance A superiority in weight, power, importance, or strength.

vestigial Remaining in a form that is small or imperfectly developed and not able to function.

vicissitude The quality or state of being changeable.

zeitgeber An environmental agent or event (such as the occurrence of light or dark) that provides the stimulus setting or resetting a biological clock of an organism.

FURTHER INFORMATION

"Feeling Our Emotions," *Scientific American*, April 1, 2005, www.scientificamerican.com/article/feeling-our-emotions/.

Wu, Jade. "Why Negative Emotions Aren't All Bad," *Scientific American*, November 5, 2019, www.scientificamerican.com/article/why-negative-emotions-arent-all-bad/.

Seubert, Janina, and Christina Regenbogen. "Subtle Multisensory Clues Reveal Other People's Emotions," *Scientific American*, March 1, 2012, www.scientificamerican.com/article/i-know-how-you-feel/.

Dobbs, David. "Mastery of Emotions," *Scientific American*, February 1, 2006, www.scientificamerican.com/article/mastery-of-emotions/.

Chen, Ingfei. "Emotion Selectively Distorts Our Recollections," *Scientific American*, January 1, 2012, www.scientificamerican.com/article/a-feeling-for-the-past/.

Wenner, Melinda. "Smile! It Could Make You Happier," *Scientific American*, September 1, 2009, www.scientificamerican.com/article/smile-it-could-make-you-happier/.

Schubert, Siri. "A Look Tells All," *Scientific American*, October 1, 2006, www.scientificamerican.com/article/a-look-tells-all/.

Mobbs, Dean, Ralph Adolphs, Michael S. Fanselow, Lisa Feldman Barrett, Joseph E. Ledoux, Kerry Ressler, Kay M. Tye and Nature Neuroscience. "On the Nature of Fear," *Scientific American*, October 10, 2019, www.scientificamerican.com/article/on-the-nature-of-fear/.

CITATIONS

1.1 Beliefs about Emotions Influence How People Feel, Act and Relate to Others by Francine Russo (November 21, 2023); 1.2 Being Empathetic Is Easier when Everyone's Doing It by Elizabeth Svoboda (September 17, 2024); 1.3 Facial Expressions Do Not Reveal Emotions by Lisa Feldman Barrett (April 27, 2022); 1.4 Too Much Emotional Intelligence Is a Bad Thing by Agata Blaszczak-Boxe (March 1, 2017); 1.5 Can You Tell Someone's Emotional State from an MRI? by Veronique Greenwood (March 1, 2017); 1.6 You Can Literally Sniff Out Other People's Inner Feelings by Marta Zaraska (December 22, 2023); 1.7 Sniffing Women's Tears Makes Men Less Aggressive by Rachel Nuwer (December 21, 2023); 1.8 Kindness Can Have Unexpectedly Positive Consequences by Amit Kumar (December 12, 2022); 1.9 There Are No Such Things as Gendered Emotions by Pragya Agarwal (June 24, 2024); 2.1 Negative Emotions Are Key to Well-Being by Tori Rodriguez (May 1, 2013); 2.2 A Newly Discovered Brain Signal Marks Recovery from Depression by Ingrid Wickelgren (September 20, 2023); 2.3 Suppressing an Onrush of Toxic Thoughts Might Improve Your Mental Health by Ingrid Wickelgren (September 20, 2023); 2.4 Outrage Fatigue Is Real. These Tips May Help by Tanya Lewis (December 30, 2024); 2.5 Can Outrage Be a Good Thing? by Victoria Spring (January 22, 2019); 2.6 Anger Can Help You Meet Your Goals by Heather Lench (February 21, 2024); 2.7 Grief Is a Learning Experience by Claudia Christine Wolf (February 27, 2024); 2.8 Shades of Grief: When Does Mourning Become a Mental Illness? by Virginia Hughes (June 1, 2011); 2.9 Election Grief Is Real. Here's How to Cope by Meghan Bartels (November 6, 2024); 3.1 Summertime Sadness Could Be a Type of Seasonal Affective Disorder by Lauren Leffer (July 3, 2024); 3.2 Fact or Fiction?: "Spring Fever" Is a Real Phenomenon by Christie Nicholson (March 22, 2007); 3.3 How I Overcame Solastalgia by Queen Essang (November 13, 2024); 3.4 I'll Bee There for You: Do Insects Feel Emotions? by Jason G. Goldman (September 30, 2016); 4.1 Personality Can Change from One Hour to the Next by Francine Russo (April 5, 2023); 4.2 Control Your Feelings in 5 Stages by Steve Ayan (January 1, 2015); 4.3 Sleep Deprivation Sometimes Relieves Depression. A New Study May Show Why by Emily Willingham (July 3, 2023); 4.4 Why Sleep Deprivation Makes You Crabby by Tori Rodriguez (March 1, 2016); 4.5 Why Sleep-Deprived People Are More Selfish and Lonely by Daisy Yuhas (October 14, 2022); 4.6 Why Just One Sleepless Night Makes People Emotionally Fragile by Eti Ben Simon (August 15, 2023); 4.7 How Humor Takes the Edge off Hard Times by Meghan Bartels (November 25, 2024); 4.8 Forcing a Smile Using Electrical Stimulation Can Boost Your Mood by Rachel Nuwer (November 20, 2024).

Each author biography was accurate at the time the article was originally published.

INDEX

S